GREECE

A guide for students of

Classical Civilisation

by

Gillian H Greef

G H GREEF

A Guide to Greece for students of Classical Civilisation

First published 1997
2nd edition 2005
3rd edition 2007 with minor revisions to pages 24 and 68.

ISBN   978-0-9532513-7-7

Published by   G H GREEF
                 Rockleigh, 11 West Ridge,
                 Frampton Cotterell,
                 Bristol,
                 BS36 2JA
                 Tel:01454 774479
                 email: gill@gillgreef.com

Printed by Ambassador Litho, 0117 965 5252

Contents

On Greek sites only official guided tours are allowed and they are expensive and usually targeted at the tourist rather than the student. This Guidebook, therefore, is designed to be your constant companion; it allows you to explore at your own speed. I hope that it will clarify what you have learnt so far in the classroom and bring all the sites to life. However, no guidebook can possibly answer all your questions, so do not be afraid to ask whenever you need help. Each section is provided with a map to follow and notes on what to look for, what to remember and what you will need to imagine.

Enjoy your week and keep your eyes open - there is a lot to see and a lot to learn!

Gillian H Greef
January 1997

I should like to thank all those who have encouraged me in the production of this guide: Dr Susan Woodford & Professor Richard Tomlinson who attempted to correct my mistakes of fact, Hilary Deighton who edited my first typescript and, of course, all those students who have used the guide and spoken well of my efforts.

GHG

To enable you to while away the hours on a coach........

THE GREEK ALPHABET (with modern pronunciation)

Capital	Small	Name	Approximate sound
A	α	alfa	cat
B	β	vita	voice
Γ	γ	gama	sugar
			yes (before "e" & "i")
Δ	δ	thelta	this
E	ε	epsilon	ten
Z	ζ	zita	zoo
H	η	ita	feet
Θ	θ	thita	thick
I	ι	yota	feet
K	κ	kapa	kin
Λ	λ	lamtha	lad
M	μ	mi	mad
N	ν	ni	nod
Ξ	ξ	ksi	box
O	ο	omikron	taut
Π	π	pi	pig
P	ρ	ro	red
Σ	σ,ς	sigma	sit (or z before some consonants)
T	τ	taf	top
Y	υ	ipsilon	feet
Φ	φ	fi	fat
X	χ	khi	loch
			hue (before "e" & "i")
Ψ	ψ	psi	lapse
Ω	ω	omega	taut

PTO

Combinations of letters

αι	t**e**n
ει	f**ee**t
οι	f**ee**t
αυ	**af**ter (before θ,κ,ξ,π,σ,τ,φ,χ.ψ) h**ave** (before other letters)
ευ	l**ef**t (before θ,κ,ξ,π,σ,τ,φ,χ,ψ) **ev**er (before other letters)
ου	m**oo**n
γγ	E**ng**land

μπ	**b** (at beginning of a word)	**mp** elsewhere
ντ	**d** (at beginning of a word)	**nd** elsewhere
γκ	**g** (at beginning of a word)	**ng** elsewhere

NOTICE that

η, ι, υ, ει, οι	are all the same in pronunciation!
αι, ε	are both pronounced the same
ο, ω	are both pronounced the same

Useful words!

παρακαλω	please
ευχαριστω	thank you
ναι	yes
οχι	no
ΤΟΥΑΛΕΤΤΑ	toilets
ΑΝΔΡΩΝ	gents
ΓΥΝΑΙΚΩΝ	ladies

GREEK HISTORY IN A NUTSHELL!

2000 BC	Mycenae small settlement	EARLY/MID HELLADIC
1600 BC	Mycenae Palace culture Gold masks, etc.	LATE HELLADIC
1300 BC	Mycenae imperial city - Agamemnon	BRONZE AGE
1250	Trojan war?	
1150	Fall of Mycenaean culture	
800	Population of Greece rising	IRON AGE
776	Olympic Games	
594	Solon	ARCHAIC
546	Peisistratos - Beginning of "culture", Tragedy, Great Panathenaia, etc.	
508	Kleisthenes	
490	Persian wars: Battle of Marathon	CLASSICAL
480	Persian wars: Battle of Salamis	
478	Delian League	
438	The Parthenon	
431	Peloponnesian War (Athens v. Sparta)	
404	Fall of Athens	
371	Defeat of Sparta by Thebes	
338	Macedon defeats Athens & Greece	HELLENISTIC
168	Kings of Pergamum donate buildings to Athens	
146	Sack of Corinth by Romans Province of Macedonia	ROMAN
86	Sack of Athens by Sulla for helping Mithridates	
44	Julius Caesar refounds Corinth	

27 BC	Province of Achaea	ROMAN
	Athens a "free" University city	
49 AD	St Paul in Greece	
117	Hadrian - the new city	
170	Pausanias - the guidebook!	
267	Invasion & sack by barbarians	
324	Constantine removes many statues to Constantinople	
395	Olympic Games ended	
529	Emperor Justinian subdues philosophy	BYZANTINE
550-700	Slavs settle in much of Greece	
c.750	Byzantines regain control of Greece	
1204	Norman & Frankish raids - castles built	
1259	Byzantines recover most of Greece Dukes of Athens (French & Italian)	
1453	Turks take Greece	TURKISH
1687	Venetian siege of Athens Destruction of Parthenon	
1821	Greek War of Independence	

HOW TO DATE A SCULPTURE

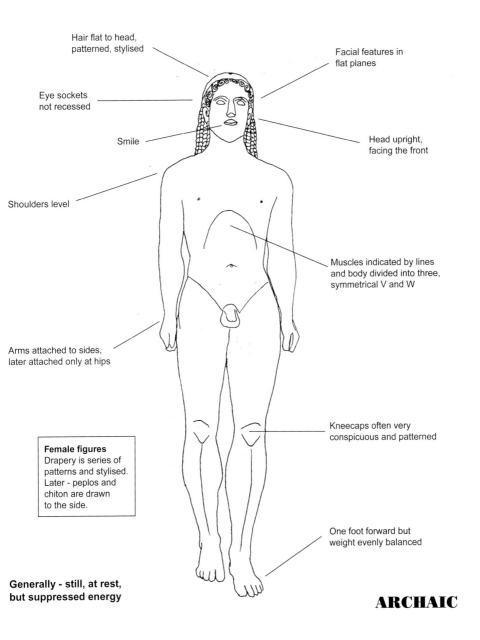

Hair flat to head, patterned, stylised

Facial features in flat planes

Eye sockets not recessed

Smile

Head upright, facing the front

Shoulders level

Muscles indicated by lines and body divided into three, symmetrical V and W

Arms attached to sides, later attached only at hips

Female figures
Drapery is series of patterns and stylised. Later - peplos and chiton are drawn to the side.

Kneecaps often very conspicuous and patterned

One foot forward but weight evenly balanced

Generally - still, at rest, but suppressed energy

ARCHAIC

CLASSICAL

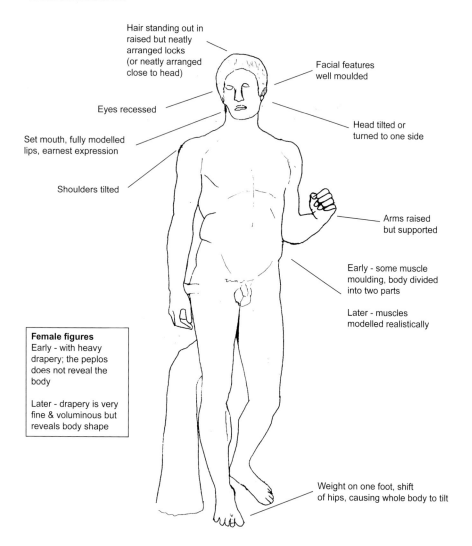

Hair standing out in raised but neatly arranged locks (or neatly arranged close to head)

Facial features well moulded

Eyes recessed

Head tilted or turned to one side

Set mouth, fully modelled lips, earnest expression

Shoulders tilted

Arms raised but supported

Early - some muscle moulding, body divided into two parts

Later - muscles modelled realistically

Female figures
Early - with heavy drapery; the peplos does not reveal the body

Later - drapery is very fine & voluminous but reveals body shape

Weight on one foot, shift of hips, causing whole body to tilt

Generally greater freedom, confidence, serenity, severity

Fifth century sculpture is heroic & idealised, presenting divine figures as majestic and aloof

All anatomical problems had been solved by the end of the fifth century.
Sculptors understood that all motion in a body is interrelated - one part cannot move without the other

Important statues were made from cast bronze: most originals have been melted down and lost.

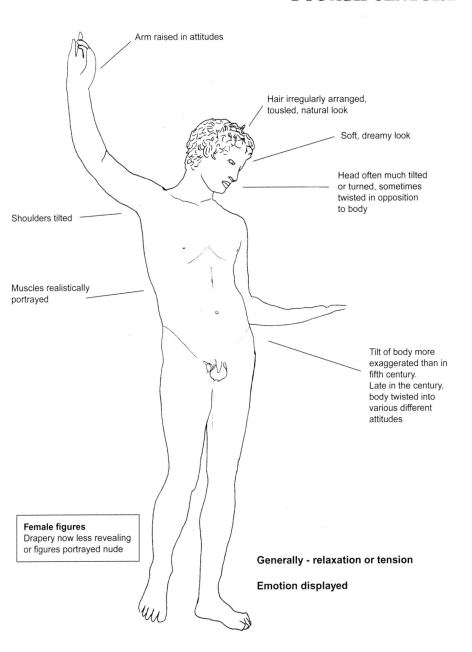

Arm raised in attitudes

Hair irregularly arranged, tousled, natural look

Soft, dreamy look

Head often much tilted or turned, sometimes twisted in opposition to body

Shoulders tilted

Muscles realistically portrayed

Tilt of body more exaggerated than in fifth century. Late in the century, body twisted into various different attitudes

Female figures
Drapery now less revealing or figures portrayed nude

Generally - relaxation or tension

Emotion displayed

Statues still made from bronze, but revival of marble statuary

THE DORIC ORDER

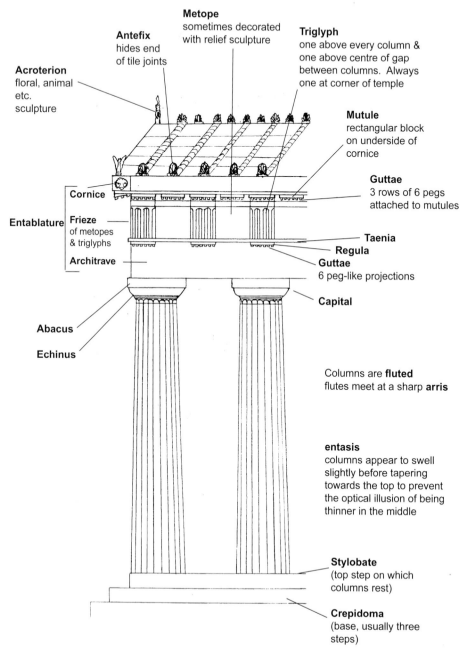

Metope
sometimes decorated with relief sculpture

Antefix
hides end of tile joints

Triglyph
one above every column & one above centre of gap between columns. Always one at corner of temple

Acroterion
floral, animal etc. sculpture

Mutule
rectangular block on underside of cornice

Cornice

Guttae
3 rows of 6 pegs attached to mutules

Entablature

Frieze
of metopes & triglyphs

Architrave

Taenia

Regula

Guttae
6 peg-like projections

Capital

Abacus

Echinus

Columns are **fluted**
flutes meet at a sharp **arris**

entasis
columns appear to swell slightly before tapering towards the top to prevent the optical illusion of being thinner in the middle

Stylobate
(top step on which columns rest)

Crepidoma
(base, usually three steps)

THE IONIC ORDER

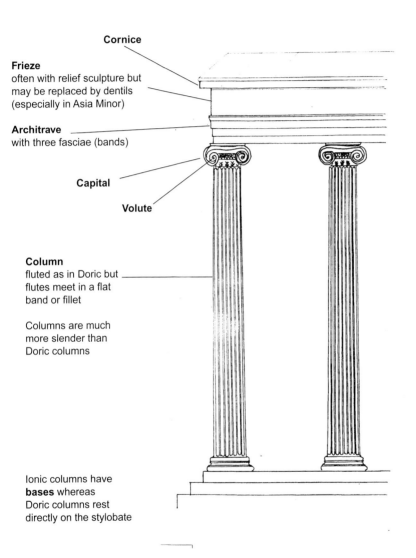

Cornice

Frieze
often with relief sculpture but
may be replaced by dentils
(especially in Asia Minor)

Architrave
with three fasciae (bands)

Capital

Volute

Column
fluted as in Doric but
flutes meet in a flat
band or fillet

Columns are much
more slender than
Doric columns

Ionic columns have
bases whereas
Doric columns rest
directly on the stylobate

Dentils

Coffers

TEMPLE PLANS

AMPHIPROSTYLE
with columns at the front
and back only

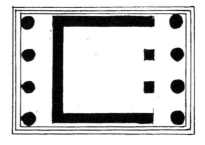

N

PERIPTERAL
with columns all round

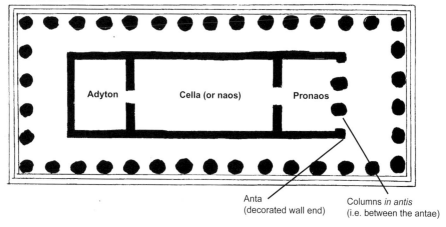

Anta
(decorated wall end)

Columns *in antis*
(i.e. between the antae)

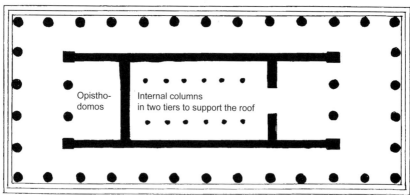

Early temples tend to be long and narrow with thick columns close together,
as early builders were uncertain of the strength of stone.

Early temples are also more likely to have an adyton or treasury.

Later builders preferred the symmetry of pronaos and opisthodomos.

14

ATHENS

National
Archaeological
Museum

M Omonia
Square

Station street

Athens street

Piraeus street

KERAMEIKOS

Ermou street

M

M Monastiraki

M

M

Temple of
Hephaistos

AGORA

Roman
market

Areopagos

ACROPOLIS

Pnyx

National Gardens

Monument of
Lysicrates

Odeion of
Herodes Atticus

Dionysiou Areopagitou

Theatre of
Dionysos

Arch of
Hadrian

Walls of Hadrian's city

M

Temple of
Zeus

Stadium

Philopappos monument

Fifth century walls

← Long walls

M = METRO

ACROPOLIS

Propylaia

Monumental gateway built 437-432
Architect was Mnesikles
Plans may have been curtailed - evidence of unfinished walls
Made of Pentelic marble and black limestone

No view of Parthenon until you emerge from Propylaia
View back to Salamis - scene of greatest triumph of Athens

NOTICE   Difference between Doric and Ionic fluting as you enter the Propylaia
            Off-centre door of "picture gallery" (used as an official dining room)

LOOK AT   Temple of Athena Nike

IMAGINE   Balustrade round edge of bastion with relief sculpture
                of Nike tying sandal etc. on the exterior
            Colour decoration on ceiling coffers

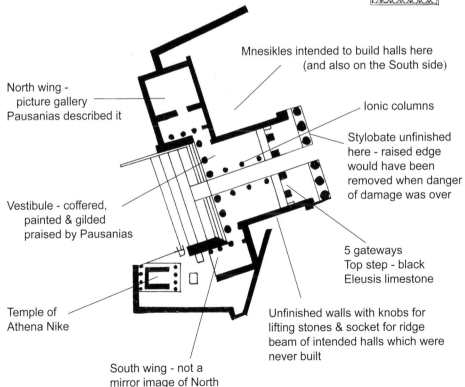

Mnesikles intended to build halls here
(and also on the South side)

North wing -
    picture gallery
Pausanias described it

Ionic columns

Stylobate unfinished
here - raised edge
would have been
removed when danger
of damage was over

Vestibule - coffered,
    painted & gilded
    praised by Pausanias

5 gateways
Top step - black
Eleusis limestone

Temple of
Athena Nike

Unfinished walls with knobs for
lifting stones & socket for ridge
beam of intended halls which were
never built

South wing - not a
mirror image of North

ACROPOLIS

	LOOK AT	First view of Parthenon (three-quarter view)

1	LOOK FOR	Traces of the statue of Athena Promachos
		    - foundations
		    - egg & tongue moulding
		Erected in 458BC as trophy of Persian wars

	IMAGINE	About 9 metres high Spear tip & helmet crest visible as approached by sea from Sounion
	FOLLOW	The route of the Panathenaic procession
2	**Turn right**	To temple of Athena Nike for sacrifice of first and best cow see notes on page 21

Return to Athena Promachos & pass between Erechtheion and Parthenon

3	**Turn left**	To offer the peplos (robe) to statue of Athena in the Erechtheion see notes on page 22
4	**Now visit**	The Acropolis museum see notes on page 24
	AT LAST....	**THE PARTHENON**
5	LOOK FIRST	From the viewpoint near the Museum
	IMAGINE	The pediment with its sculpture of the birth of Athena The whole temple complete and brightly coloured see detailed notes on page 23
	Finally	Walk between the Parthenon and edge of the Acropolis, if you can

6	LOOK AT	The foundations and platform of the temple begun in the 480s
		    & burnt (when still unfinished) by the Persians in 480BC.
		        Extended at NW corner for facade of 8 columns instead of 6
		The reconstruction of the roofing

	LOOK DOWN	To the theatre of Dionysos
	LOOK FOR	Deep pits revealing earlier walls Steps to west front of Parthenon with cuttings for votive offerings

7 **Sanctuary of Artemis**

    Votive offerings were found here including a "Little Bear"- remember Lysistrata

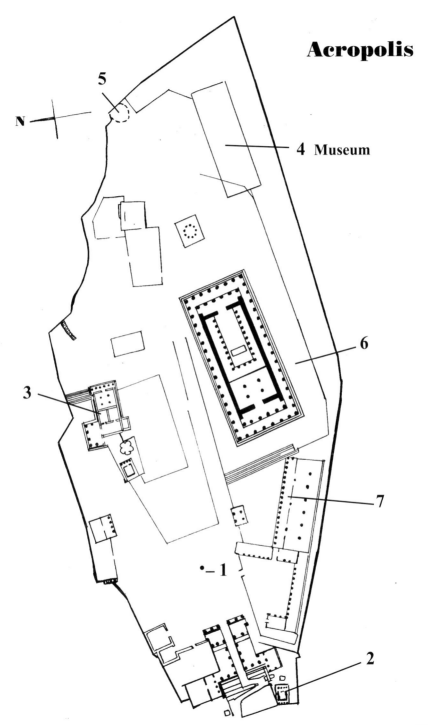

Acropolis

N

5

4 Museum

6

3

7

•– 1

2

TEMPLE OF ATHENA NIKE

Built 427-424
Pentelic marble

The architect was said to have been Kallikrates but he probably built the little sanctuary
concealed under the temple.

LOOK FOR: Altar - first & best cow at Panathenaic festival sacrificed here
Monolithic shafts (= one piece of stone - column on left repaired!)
Capitals - decoration
Corner capitals - volutes twisted so that volutes face both ways
Frieze   - divinities on East front
               - battles on the other three sides
Square piers instead of columns *in antis*

IMAGINE   Statue inside - pomegranate and helmet
Complete temple with pediments
Balustrade round edge of bastion

LOOK AT   View to Salamis

OR IMAGINE IT!!!!!

ERECHTHEION

Between Parthenon and Erechtheion

LOOK FOR	Foundations of old Temple of Athena
LOOK AT	Erechtheion from all sides
NOTICE	Two distinct ground levels

LOOK EAST 6 columns - Pentelic marble
       (one is a cast of the column in British Museum)
      Decoration on capitals and bases
      Doorway & windows were removed when became church
      Good examples of mouldings - palmette & lotus }
                egg & tongue } = anthemion
                cyma reversa }

East

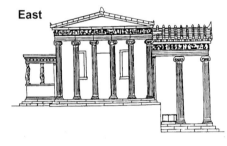

West

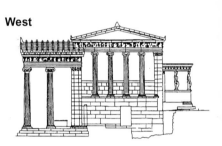

LOOK NORTH Largest columns
        Ornate decoration on capitals and bases
        Frieze - black Eleusinian limestone } frieze looked like
        Holes for attaching white marble figures } a Wedgwood vase
        Coffered ceiling
        Hole in floor to show marks of thunderbolt
        Hole above in ceiling
        Doorway richly decorated - which mouldings?

LOOK WEST   Olive planted in 1917
        Engaged columns above blank wall
        Cecrops' tomb   - foundations in SW corner
                 - one huge block spans tomb

LOOK SOUTH Korai ("Caryatids") - casts - weight on which leg?
                    - hair long to strengthen neck
        Entablature   - fasciae & rosettes
                 - dentils
        Wall mouldings along plain wall

IMAGINE   Complete temple including colour

PARTHENON

LOOK AT   Regular Doric entablature - especially at NE corner - reconstruction
Taenia, regulae, mutules, guttae, metopes, triglyphs etc.
Lions' heads at corners

LOOK FOR   Optical refinements:
             Curve of stylobate - best seen from NE corner
             Corner columns thicker
             Varied spacing of columns on front (look at corners)
             Spacing of triglyphs at corners
             Columns leaning inward
             Entasis - look slantwise between columns at sky

IMAGINE   Antefixes and acroteria on roof
Colour
Pediments   - East   - birth of Athena
                     - West   - contest of Poseidon & Athena

LOOK AT   Metopes - East - battle with giants
                     - West - battle with Amazons

IMAGINE   Frieze - high up over walls and porches within the peristyle

INSIDE

REMEMBER   Pronaos has 6 prostyle columns (i.e. no columns *in antis*)
Opisthodomos like pronaos
2 chambers inside
       Larger held statue & had 2-storey colonnades in U shape
       Smaller was treasury & had 4 Ionic columns

IMAGINE   Statue made by Pheidias

           Panathenaic procession and festival

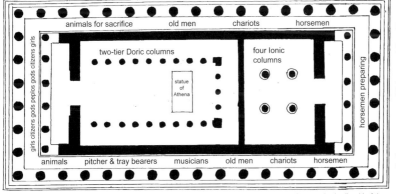

East end - the front of the temple

N

West end - the 'back' of the
temple but seen first as you
approach from the Propylaia

ACROPOLIS MUSEUM

The new museum opens in 2008.

I hope you will be able to find all the exhibits listed below which were on display in the old Acropolis museum. There should also be new displays including what was found as the museum was being built - life in Athens 2500 years ago.

Artemis from Parthenon frieze

LOOK FOR   **Archaic sculpture**
Moschophoros
Peplos kore (540-530BC)
Chios kore - no.675 (530-520BC)
Kore of Antenor - no.681 (530-510BC)
Euthydikos kore - no.686 (490-480BC)
Sculpture from Old Temple of Athena pediment

NOTICE   Methods by which arms were attached to korai

LOOK AT   The eyes of the korai (some show traces of colour)

LOOK FOR   **Early Classical sculpture**
Relief of Mourning Athena (470-450BC)
Kritian boy (490-480BC)
Plinth with feet (essential for marble statues)

Classical Sculpture
Original Korai of Erechtheion ("Caryatids")
Nike untying sandal from parapet of "Athena Nike"

Lenormant relief of trireme

Parthenon sculpture
Kekrops group
Selene torso
Poseidon torso
and metopes

Parthenon frieze
Poseidon, Apollo, Artemis & Aphrodite
Youths and oxen
Youths and rams
Jar carriers

LOOK FOR   Drill holes under hem of dress on reliefs to add shadows
on block with sheep on Parthenon frieze

MONUMENT OF PHILOPAPPOS

Built 114-116 AD
Distinguished career as Athenian citizen and Roman consul

PNYX

Three periods of construction
        500BC - seating faced North with clear view to Acropolis

IMAGINE   Pericles persuading Athenians to rebuild the temples on the Acropolis

        403BC - reversed in time of 30 tyrants
        4th Century BC - grand plan
                Colossal retaining wall helped to form auditorium
                No evidence of seating
                Single entrance was flight of steps on North side
                Three-stepped platform for speakers
                Above platform is foundation for altar
                Farther up, foundations for stoas

> The Prytaneis got up in the middle of their dinner; some began to clear the stall-holders out of the Agora and others sent for the Generals and summoned the trumpeter. The whole city was in uproar; and at dawn, the Prytaneis convened the Boule in its chamber, and you set out for the Assembly. Before the Boule had finished drafting the agenda, the whole People was already seated up there.
>
> Demosthenes

ROCK OF THE AREOPAGOS

BEWARE OF SLIPPERY ROCKS!!!!!

LOOK AT   View of Agora
                    View of Acropolis
                    View of Pnyx

NORTH SIDE OF THE ACROPOLIS

Just past the cafe

High up .... at the top of the Acropolis

LOOK AT   Old drums from temples destroyed by the Persians
                    used in Acropolis wall
                Architrave, triglyphs and metopes from old temple reassembled in
                    5th century after the Persian destruction (as a war memorial??
                    or as a reminder never to let the Persians return)

SOUTH SIDE OF ACROPOLIS

Monument of Lysikrates

334BC

"Lysikrates of Kikyna, son of Lysitheides, was choregos; the tribe of Akamantis won the victory with a chorus of boys; Theon played the flute; Lysiades of Athens trained the chorus; Euainetos was archon".

It was the custom to dedicate the tripods won in the Festival of Dionysos to the god. They were often placed on monuments like this one.

Theatre of Dionysos

Rebuilt in stone 342BC.
Much modified in Roman times.

REMEMBER	Aeschylus, Sophocles, Euripides, Aristophanes City Dionysia, Lenaia
REMEMBER	Crowns presented to distinguished citizens here Orphans of Athenian soldiers paraded on reaching manhood Presentation of Delian League tribute

LOOK AT	Seats	- throne of priest of Dionysos in centre
		- front row, made of Pentelic marble, inscribed with names of priests or notable citizens
		- rest of seats Piraeus limestone
	Orchestra	- Roman in shape
	Scaena	- also Roman - reliefs 2nd century AD
		- foundations of earlier structures behind
	Monument of a victorious choregos above	

From the top of the theatre...

Walk round the base of the Acropolis

Asklepieion

Dedicated 418BC.
Worship of Asklepios introduced in plague of 429BC.
Healing continued into Christian era - church.

Odeion of Herodes Atticus

Built in honour of his wife who died 160AD.
Some people believe it was roofed but would have been a massive achievement.
Julius Atticus found a huge sum of money in an old house.
He tactfully told emperor, then used it for public works & to educate his son, Herodes.
Herodes was consul at Rome, then retired to Athens and continued public works.

ROMAN ATHENS

Athens was the great city of Hadrian

Arch of Hadrian marks beginning of enlargement of city walls
"This is Athens, the ancient city of Theseus"
"This is the city of Hadrian and not of Theseus"
Inscriptions on either side of Arch

Temple of Olympian Zeus
Foundations for huge Doric temple
        laid by Peisistratos or Hippias in 6th century BC
Resumed & largely built in 2nd century BC
Completed by Hadrian - 130AD
8×20 columns
Corinthian
Two rows of columns on sides
Three rows on front & back
Pentelic marble
Fallen column shows construction of base

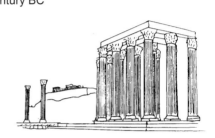

Stadium
Faithfully restored 1896 for Modern Olympics
Corresponds to description of Pausanias
Pentelic marble

Roman Market
Unlike Greek Agora - symmetrical in plan
Open rectangle with colonnades on all sides
Principal entrance at centre of West end - double Doric porch
At opposite end - porch off-centre leads to Tower of Winds
Public loo (ancient!) near entrance (modern!)

Tower of Winds
Early first century BC
Elaborate water clock
Originally had bronze weathercock in form of Triton
8 Winds carved on relevant sides

Library of Hadrian - 130 AD
West end with entrance - Corinthian colonnade
Inside rectangular court with colonnades
East end had 2-3 storey building which housed library
Can see some of outer wall and outer colonnade on West side

KERAMEIKOS

LOOK AT   The view from the mound just to the right of the entrance

IMAGINE   Athenians preparing for the Panathenaic procession
The pride of an Athenian as he looked on

Street of tombs - begun 394 BC
The "best"place for a tomb - Pericles, etc.

- plain stelai with palmette anthemion
- stelai with reliefs in a frame
- architectural tombs
- columns with animal on top
- marble lekythoi (one handle)
- loutrophoroi (two handles)

Wall of Themistokles
Bottom course (mud brick on stone footing)
Three levels above:
    394 BC - Conon
    338 BC - Lykourgos
    500 AD - Justinian

Dipylon gate
Rebuilt end of 4th century
Favourite way to Piraeus

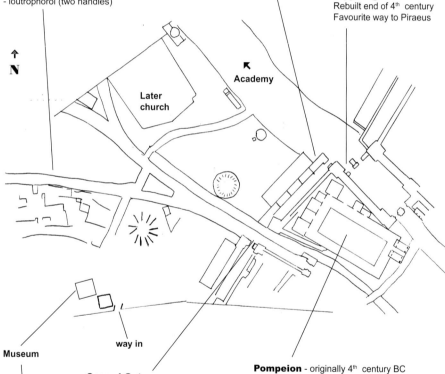

N

Later church

Academy

way in

Museum

Sacred Gate
Sacred way to Eleusis passed
   through it.
Eridanos brook in vaulted channel.

LOOK FOR
Recently discovered kouros
Ostraka
Stelai - grave stones

Pompeion - originally 4th century BC
Used for preparation for processions
Rooms on N & W were for 7, 11 or 15
    VIPs dining, according to room size
Mudbrick/stone - marble gateway at East
Sulla destroyed it.
Massively rebuilt as Roman warehouse
with concrete foundations.

LOOK AT   metal clamps to join blocks
                wheel ruts
                holes for door fittings

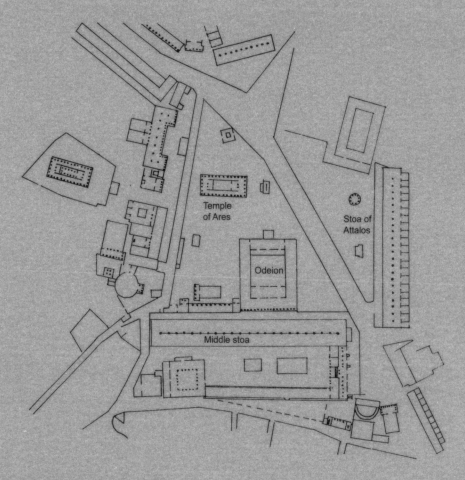

Temple
of Ares

Stoa of
Attalos

Odeion

Middle stoa

2ⁿᵈ CENTURY AD

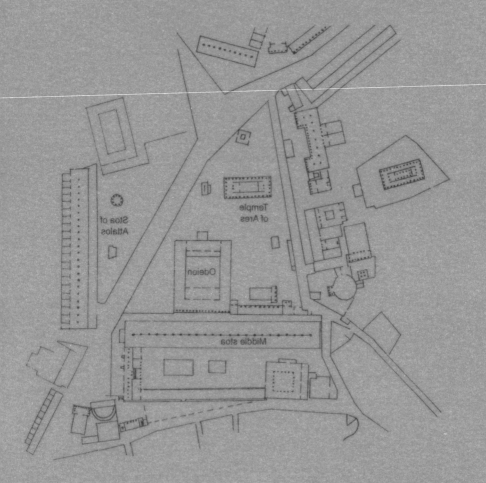

Temple
of Ares

Stoa of
Attalos

Odeion

Middle stoa

2nd CENTURY AD

THE AGORA

5ᵗʰ CENTURY BC

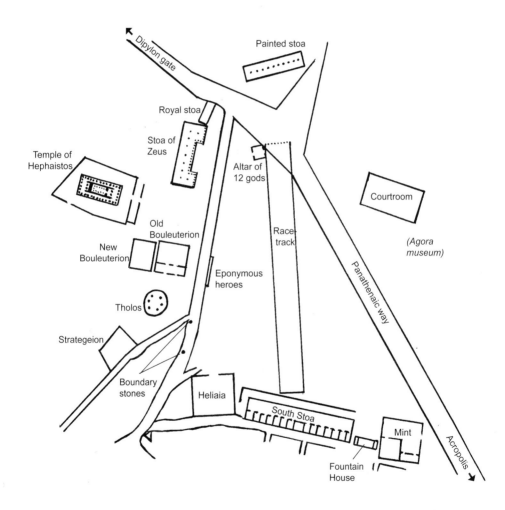

AGORA

IMAGINE   Ostracisms
               Socrates debating
               St Paul preaching

USE PLANS to disentangle the ruinous chaos!!
The Agora was flattened when Athens was reduced in size - clear ground was
   needed in front of the new city wall for safety.

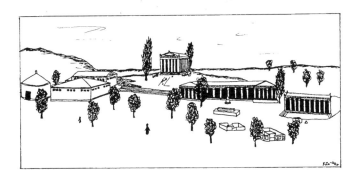

The Agora

Temple of Hephaistos

Built 449-444 BC

REMEMBER   Viewpoint from Agora all important
               Bronzesmiths' workshops were found in this area
               Temple was surrounded by a precinct (as always)
               Formal garden was added in Hellenistic times

DIMENSIONS: 45×104 feet
               6×13 columns
                   19 feet high
                   3'4" diameter
               Entablature   6'6" high
               Cella   26 feet wide

LOOK AT   Pentelic marble
               Limestone lowest step
               Coffers in ceiling of colonnade
               Inner Ionic carved frieze - frieze longer at East end than at West
               Metopes at East end (10 on front and 4 on each side)
               Ionic mouldings instead of regulae & guttae in porches

IMAGINE   Pediment sculpture in Parian marble
               Interior with two rows of two-tier columns plus one at the back
                  - replaced by barrel vault when the temple became a church!

31

Metopes of the Temple of Hephaistos

NORTH-EAST Theseus

Minotaur

Marathonian
Bull

Sinis

Prokrustes

EAST Herakles

Nemean
Lion

Hydra of
Lerna

Hind of
Keryneia

Erymanthean
boar

Horses of
Diomedes

Kerberos

Amazons

Eurytion

Geryon

Apples of
Hesperides

SOUTH-EAST Theseus

Sow of
Krommyon

Skiron

Kerkyon

Periphetes

IN THE AGORA

LOOK FOR   **Boundary stone** - near junction of Great Drain

Simon's shop directly behind (easy to identify from almost triangular ground plan)

IMAGINE   Socrates chatting

LOOK FOR   **Tholos**

                               6 columns to support roof

                       New Bouleuterion
                       NW of Tholos on platform

                       Old Bouleuterion
                       Square building

                       Great Drain
                       Limestone polygonal blocks
                       Led to Eridanos brook

LOOK AT   **Eponymous Heroes** - the public notice board
                       4th century base in front of Old Bouleuterion
                       It was moved here in the fourth century

LOOK AT   **Stoa of Zeus** - 430 BC
                       Winged stoa
                       Doric outside
                       Ionic inside
                       Acroteria were Victories
                       Decorated with paintings, according to Pausanias

LOOK AT   **Panathenaic way**

IMAGINE   The Panathenaic procession and competitions

If you have time, in the South of the Agora:

LOOK FOR   **Fountain house**
                Mint
                South Stoa with 15 rooms
                        Probably for boards of officials - including dining rooms
                        Inscription on Weights & Measures found here

AGORA MUSEUM
Reconstruction of 2nd century BC Stoa of Attalos
                         - part of old structure incorporated into the new

LOOK FOR   Hemlock pots & tiny bust of Socrates
                Hobnails   
                Mould for casting bronze
                Weights and measures
                Ballots
                Klepsydra (water clock to time speeches in court)
                Kleroterion (allotment machine for choosing jurors)
                Activities on vases
                Baby's high-chair
                Ostraka (broken pottery for ostracism votes)
                Cooking pots   
                Obols - note how small they are

Outside the Agora, across the railway in Adrianou street:

LOOK FOR   **Royal Stoa**
                        8 Doric columns 480 BC
                        Stone for swearing oaths of office
                        Wings added later

REMEMBER SOCRATES & EUTHYPHRO

On the other side of Adrianou street:

LOOK FOR   **Painted Stoa** - founded in fifth century BC
                        Here Zeno taught his disciples - the Stoics
                        Decorated with battle scenes (Marathon, Troy, etc.)
                        Described by Pausanias

NATIONAL MUSEUM

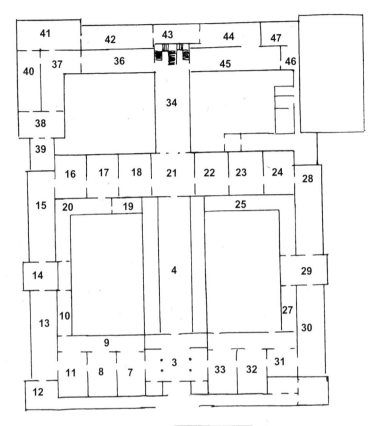

Some suggestions:

Room 4 Shaft graves at Mycenae

LOOK AT   **Dagger blades** - flesh gold, clothes silver
             Nestor's cup (doves on handle)
             Mask of Agamemnon
             Warrior vase
             Linear B tablets

SCULPTURE
Follow the rooms in numerical order to see the development of sculpture:

LOOK FOR   Plinths which form part of marble statues (impossible without)
             Bases into which plinths are sunk
             Bronze statues need no plinths so stand straight on bases

ARCHAIC SCULPTURE

Room 8	Kouros from Sounion (huge) [600BC]	2720
Room 11	Apollo from Melos [c 550BC]	1558
	Phrasikleia by Aristion of Paros [540BC]	4890
	- colour, earrings, holding lotus flower - symbol of eternity	
	Phrasikleia's brother	4889
Room 13	Anavyssos kouros [520BC]	3851
	Aristodikos [500BC]	3938
	Palaestra scenes [510BC]	3476

CLASSICAL SCULPTURE

Room 15	Omphalos Apollo [460-450BC]	45
	Zeus of Artemision [460BC]	15161
Room 20	Varvakeion Athena (miniature of Pheidias' statue)	
Room 21	Diadoumenos [430BC]	1826

FUNERAL STELAI

Room 18	Hegeso (end of 5th century BC)
	Hoplite lost at sea - in top right corner, rest would have been blue!
Room 23	Stele from Ilissos 869

BRONZE SCULPTURES

Room 21	Horse and jockey of Artemision [140BC]	15177
Room 28	Youth from Antikythera [340BC]	13396
	Marathon boy [335-325BC]	15118
Room 31	Augustus [late 1st century BC]	

ARCHITECTURAL SCULPTURE

Room 22   Temple of Asklepios at Epidauros
                - Pediments: East - Fall of Troy, West - Greeks v. Amazons

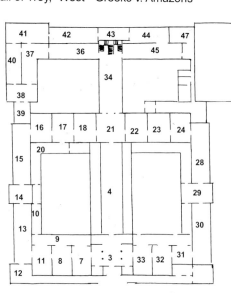

OTHER ITEMS OF INTEREST

Vases   Black figure,
                 Red figure
                 White ground, etc.

Have you seen?

Holes where metal was attached
Remains of paint on statues
Where hands were attached to statues
Eyes - coloured stone

ATHENS TO DELPHI

LOOK FOR
      Quarries - Pentelic marble etc.
      Olives
      Vines
      River channels with little water

Mount Kithairon
      (on the left, behind Thebes)
        - Oedipus exposed here
        - Pentheus torn to pieces

Thebes
      - Main city of ancient Boiotia
      - Home of ...??

A place where three roads meet!!!!!

Osios Loukas
      - see over

Arakhova
      - Mountain town on slopes of Parnassos
      - Famous for hand-woven carpets
      - Good views to and from it

As we approach Delphi:

LOOK FOR
      Sanctuary of Athena on the left
      Monument most often shown on postcards - the **Tholos**
      Gymnasium below

LOOK FOR
      Kastalian spring on the right, close to the road

LOOK UP
      At the Phaidriades
        - the cliffs which tower over the sanctuary and spring

It may be possible to walk back to view these more fully in the evening

OSIOS LOUKAS

Monastery of hermit Blessed Luke c 950 AD (not St Luke the Evangelist)
In addition to having intellectual gifts he performed miracles and his prophecies made
him famous all over the Byzantine world.

Two churches joined together, the earlier, dedicated to the Theotokos, the mother of
God, was built in the later 10th century & the later, the Katholikon, in the early 11th.

On left, as you enter the monastery, is a spring with healing properties used by Luke.

Katholikon

LOOK AT   Entrance porch (Narthex) with...
                          mosaics probably made by artists from Constantinople
                 Main domed nave - a complex cross in square shape
                 More mosaics

Mosaics in Byzantine churches follow a strict pattern. Christ in the dome,
          archangels below, then prophets and apostles, then scenes from the life of
          Christ, and below these, the earth with saints and monks.

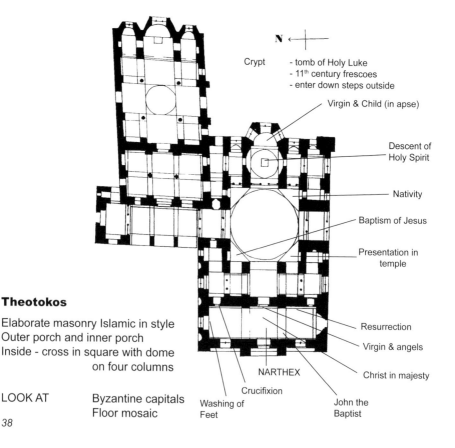

N

Crypt   - tomb of Holy Luke
         - 11th century frescoes
         - enter down steps outside

Virgin & Child (in apse)

Descent of
Holy Spirit

Nativity

Baptism of Jesus

Presentation in
temple

Theotokos

Elaborate masonry Islamic in style
Outer porch and inner porch
Inside - cross in square with dome
          on four columns

Resurrection

Virgin & angels

Christ in majesty

LOOK AT   Byzantine capitals
                 Floor mosaic

NARTHEX

Crucifixion
Washing of
Feet

John the
Baptist

DELPHI

The centre of the world.
Originally sacred to Mother Earth who was guarded by her serpent son, Pytho.
There was an oracle here from the very beginning.
When Apollo came to Delphi, he killed the serpent and took over the sanctuary.

> It is said that the earliest shrine of Apollo was built of laurel with branches brought from the grove
> at Tempe. This shrine must have been in the form of a hut.
>
> Pausanias

Delphi became independent in 6th century BC, but always had political problems.
It was notorious for appearing to be pro-Persian in the Persian Wars & was pro-Spartan
in the Peloponnesian War.

THE ORACLE

Consultations only held once a month & not at all in November, December & January.
It is possible that on other days, people could draw lots for a yes/no answer.
There could be a long queue!
Some cities and individuals had the right of **promanteia** - the right to jump the queue
- usually because of their generosity to the sanctuary.
Otherwise, the order for consulting the oracle was determined by lot.

> I have heard it said that some shepherds looking after their herds first came upon this oracle
> and became possessed by the vapour and prophesied by the power of Apollo.
>
> Pausanias

To Consult the oracle.....

Purify in Kastalian spring outside sanctuary
[wash hair (whole body if crime was murder)]
Sacrifice a goat [it should tremble if it was to be a successful day]
Wait turn in the temple
Hand in question on a lead tablet [many have been found]

The Pythia (the priestess, a peasant woman over 50)

Purified herself in the Kastalian spring
Drank the waters from the spring of Kassotis
Munched laurel leaves
Sat on tripod over a chasm
Intoxicated by fumes
Uttered incoherent sounds
Interpreted by poet/secretary

The answer was cryptic and often confusing ....

Croesus of Lydia was told he would destroy a great Empire
if he attacked Persia; .... he did: ... his own!

Themistokles and the "wooden walls". He realised that the
wooden walls which would provide Athens with safety in the
Persian wars were their ships, not the fortifications of the
Acropolis.

"Is there anyone wiser than Socrates?" No! Socrates
understood that he was wiser than others because he realised
his own ignorance.

BUT ... Strabo says Delphi's oracle had the reputation of being the most truthful.

REMEMBER   Aigeus in Medea has been to Delphi to ask how to have children
                Oedipus sends to Delphi to find out what is causing the plague

THE PYTHIAN GAMES
Commemorated the killing of Pytho.
Began with sacrifice & play recalling killing of Pytho,
        then procession & further sacrifice on next day.
Became major festival in 582 BC - every four years like Olympic Games.
Musical contests including hymns in honour of Apollo.
Athletic contests.
Chariot races on the plain.
Prize was a wreath of laurel.

> The earliest contest the Delphic people remember and the one where a prize was first offered was for
> singing a hymn to the god. Chrysothemis of Crete, whose father Karmanor is said to have purified Apollo,
> sang and won a victory.
>
> In the third year after the forty-eighth Olympics, the League offered a prize for singing with the harp in
> the usual way but that year they added a competition in flute playing.
>
> This was also the first time they gave prizes for athletes, with all the Olympic competitions except the
> four-horsed chariots, and adding a boys' race on the long course and on the double course. At the sec-
> ond Pythian games, the challenge was not to compete for prizes; from then on a wreath of laurel was
> the victor's crown.
>
> Pausanias

If you walk towards the sanctuaries of Apollo & Athena in the evening:

LOOK UP   At the Phaidriades - cliffs which tower over the sanctuary & spring

LOOK FOR   Sanctuary of Apollo on steep hillside on left
                Kastalian spring beyond, close to the road.

LOOK FOR   Sanctuary of Athena on the right
                The **Tholos** - use unknown!!!!
                Gymnasium below

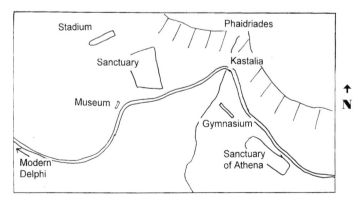

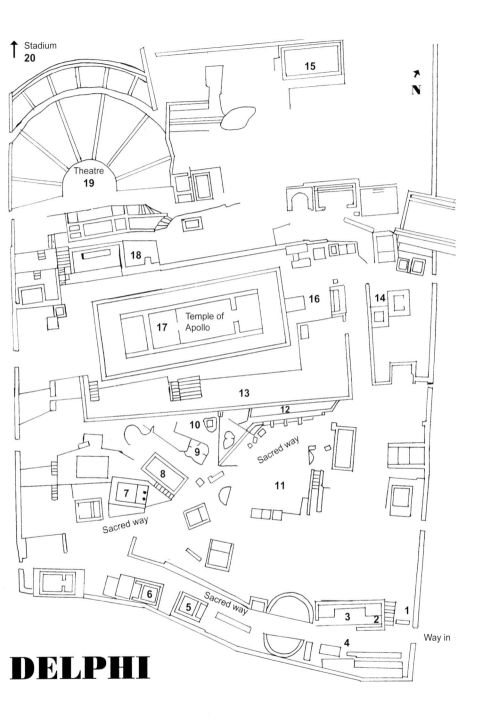

Stadium
20

15

N

Theatre
19

18

16

14

17 Temple of
Apollo

13

12

10

9

Sacred way

8

11

7

Sacred way

6

5 Sacred way

3

2

1

4

Way in

DELPHI

SANCTUARY OF APOLLO

The sanctuary was surrounded by a wall but there were at least eleven entrances. We enter by the main entrance, following the route of the **Sacred Way.**

Inside the site (but outside the sanctuary)

NOTICE   The late Roman market place with its reconstructed colonnade
       (there were shops on two sides
            - useful for would-be visitors to the sanctuary)

NOW ENTER THE SANCTUARY

As you entered the sanctuary, you were confronted by an array of monuments, mostly erected by cities competing with one another to commemorate famous victories!! Little is left but a confused mass of masonry so ...

IMAGINE **[1 on plan]** **Bull of Kerkyra** (Corfu)

As you go into the sanctuary, there is a Bronze Bull by Theopropos of Aigina, dedicated by the people of Corfu. The legend is that a bull in Corfu had abandoned the pasture and deserted the other cattle; it went bellowing down to the sea and the same thing happened every day. To find out why, the herdsman came down to the shore and saw a fantastic number of tunny-fish. He showed these fish to the people in the city, and, when, in spite of taking great trouble, they could not catch them, they sent to enquire at Delphi. In consequence, they slaughtered the bull to Poseidon and immediately after the sacrifice they caught the fish, and the dedications at Olympia and at Delphi are a tithe of the catch.

                     Pausanias

IMAGINE **[2]** Offering of Arcadians (hurrah for the defeat of Sparta - 369BC)
      [3] Monument of the Admirals (hurrah for defeat of Athens - 403BC)
      [4] Monument of Athenians 460 BC - statues by Pheidias of the
          Eponymous Heroes who gave their names to the ten tribes,
            + statues of Miltiades (leader at Marathon), Athene & Apollo

All these are very difficult to make out so **move on to...**

TREASURY OF SIKYON [5]

LOOK AT   Foundations which date from early 5th century
        Foundations of earlier buildings were found inside
        Metopes in museum are from earlier building - 560 BC

TREASURY OF SIPHNOS   [6]

Built with tithe of profits from gold mines in 525 BC
Remains are in the museum

IMAGINE   Columns *in antis* in form of Caryatids
        Frieze of Parian marble on all four sides
        Statues on pediment (Herakles and the tripod)

TREASURY OF THE ATHENIANS [7]

Possibly built just after the battle of Marathon but may well be a little earlier.
Rebuilt in 1906 (in the 19th century it was a pawn shop).

LOOK AT   Doric treasury with two columns *in antis*
                    Metopes of Theseus and Herakles
                    Inscriptions all over walls:
                                - Some record embassies
                                - Others record decrees
                                - Two hymns to Apollo with music!!

IMAGINE   Trophy on platform to left commemorating victory over the Persians

All around were other **treasuries** but these are difficult to make out.
Every city was eager to outdo its rivals!!

Next to the Treasury of the Athenians:

LOOK AT   [8]   Foundations of the **Bouleuterion** (council house)

Now we reach the most ancient part of the sanctuary

LOOK AT   [9]   The **rock of the Sibyl** (a large boulder)
                        This was the seat of the original oracle

IMAGINE   [10]   The **Sphinx of Naxos** on its tall Ionic column

LOOK FOR   Pieces of its column lying around.
                        Inscriptions telling of right of **promanteia**

LOOK AT   [11]   The **threshing floor**
                        Where the play recalling the killing of Pytho was reenacted

THE STOA OF THE ATHENIANS [12]

Built to display the trophies of Salamis.....
        .....the ropes from Xerxes' bridge over the Hellespont & the prows of the ships.

LOOK AT   Colonnade of Parian marble Ionic columns
                        Architrave and roof must have been of wood
                        On top step was a dedicatory inscription

LOOK AT   [13]   **Polygonal wall** built about 548 BC
                        Structure very good against earthquakes
                        Over 800 inscriptions on wall, mostly about freeing slaves

TRIPOD OF PLATAIA [14]

Dedicated by the 31 states who fought & defeated the Persians at Plataia in 479 BC

IMAGINE   Three intertwined bronze serpents supporting gold tripod
                        (one serpent survives in Istanbul,
                        taken by Constantine to decorate his city)

LOOK FOR   [15]   The **Lesche of Knidos**
                        - club house for visitors from Knidos
                        Pausanias describes the paintings inside

LOOK AT   [16]   **Altar of Chios**
                        Black and white marble altar
                        Inscription on base recording right
                            of **promanteia** (jumping the queue)

The Tripod
of
Plataea

TEMPLE OF APOLLO [17]

The first grand temple was built in 548 BC.
It was destroyed by earthquake in 373 BC and rebuilt on same plan.

LOOK AT   Foundations and a few columns
                  6×15 columns

IMAGINE   Mottos inscribed in porch "know yourself", "nothing in excess"
                  Priestess (Pythia) sitting on her tripod

IMAGINE   [18]   **The Charioteer** found just above the temple

THE THEATRE [19]

Built in 4th century BC and restored by Romans
Seats were white Parnassos limestone

From top of theatre

LOOK AT   **VIEW OF SANCTUARY**

Climb the hill to reach

THE STADIUM [20]

The stadium has its present form courtesy of Herodes Atticus, the Athenian who built
    much in Roman times & was rewarded by being made consul in mid 2nd century AD.

LOOK AT   Start and finish lines
                  Lane markers (holes for posts)
                  Platform for presidents

DELPHI MUSEUM

Rooms are not visibly numbered now but I have used the old system as a reference.

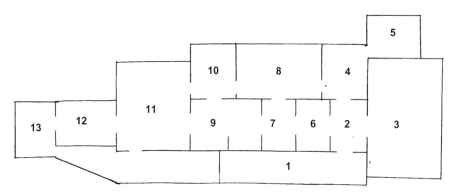

Room 3

LOOK AT   **The Sphinx of Naxos** (right of **promanteia** was inscribed on base)
Caryatid from porch of Siphnian treasury (525 BC)

LOOK AT   **Frieze & pediments from Siphnian treasury**

NOTICE   The archaic style of the sculpture

EAST PEDIMENT
Contest between Herakles and Apollo for Delphic tripod.
Zeus (or Hermes) is in the middle.
Apollo, restrained by Artemis on the left.
Herakles on the right.

NOTICE   Solutions to problem of pediment shape:- Zeus in centre, then
gods, then goddesses, then men, getting gradually smaller
Centre is successful, sides less so

EAST FRIEZE
Battle of Greeks and Trojans over a dead warrior
On the left are the pro-Trojan gods - Ares, Aphrodite, Artemis and Apollo.
Then, Zeus is seated on a throne.
In the gap, Thetis was probably begging Zeus for help for her son, Achilles.
On the right are the pro-Greek gods - Poseidon, Athene, Hera and Demeter.
The battle itself took up the rest of the frieze.

NOTICE   The similarity of the seated figures
The repetition of patterns for decorative effect
Repeated verticals and horizontals

NORTH FRIEZE
Battle of gods and giants
The giants are shown as hoplite soldiers in full armour!
On the left is Hephaistos with two sacks, probably his bellows.
Then, two goddesses and two giants.
Then Herakles (with lion skin) fighting a giant.
Then Cybele in her chariot pulled by lions.
The lion is taking a bite out of a giant!!!
Then Apollo and Artemis shooting 3 giants.
      (note the quiver on her back)
Between them, a giant runs away.

NOTICE   Tidy overlapping rows of giants
                Pose of fleeing giant
                Friendly lion!
                Colour

Room 4

LOOK AT   **Kleobis & Biton** - archaic statues by [Poly]medes of Argos (c600BC)
                Metopes from treasury of Sikyon - the Argonauts, Europa & the bull,
                      Castor & Pollux, the Calydonian boar

Room 5
The finds in this room, were discovered near the threshing floor. They were probably
    buried in the mid-fifth century BC after a disastrous fire in the sanctuary.

LOOK AT   Silver bull from late 6th century
                Head of a man in gold and ivory - a clue to Pheidias' gold and ivory
                      statues in the Parthenon & temple of Zeus at Olympia
                Plates of gold to attach to body of statue as in Parthenon

Room 6

LOOK AT   Metopes from **Treasury of the Athenians**

Room 7

LOOK AT   Hymn to Apollo with music from walls of Treasury

Room 9

LOOK AT   **Bronze statuette** of girl with bowl balanced on her head - incense
                    burner (notice her knee breaking lines of folds of dress)

Room 11

LOOK AT   **Six statues** from one monument of 330s BC
                Agias is almost certainly a copy of a bronze by Lysippos

Room 13

LOOK AT   **The Charioteer** (480BC) - without his chariot and four horses!

DELPHI TO OLYMPIA

Naupaktos
- Important strategic position on Corinthian Gulf
- Captured by Athenians in 455 BC
- Spartan Helots who had rebelled were settled here by Athenians
- Important in Peloponnesian War
- Fortified by Venetians in fourteenth century AD
- Then called Lepanto
- Recaptured by Turks in 1500
- 1571 last great battle of oar-powered ships: Venetians defeated Turks

    TO LOOK FOR
- Small mediaeval harbour
- Venetian fortress

Patras
- Largest town in Peloponnese
- High status in Roman Empire
- Site of martyrdom of St Andrew
- Archaeological museum
- Little else to see except huge 19th /20th century cathedral.

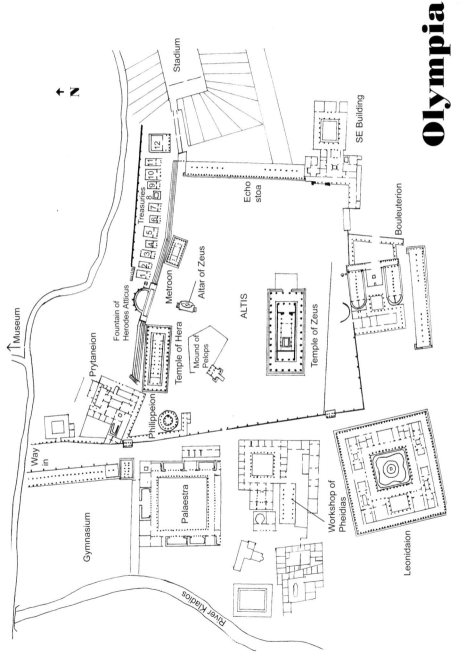

Olympia

Museum

N

Gymnasium

Palaestra

River Kladios

Way in

Prytaneion

Philippeion

Fountain of Herodes Atticus

Treasures

1 2 3 4 5 6 7 8 9 10 11

12

Metroon

Altar of Zeus

Temple of Hera

Mound of Pelops

ALTIS

Stadium

Echo stoa

SE Building

Bouleuterion

Temple of Zeus

Workshop of Pheidias

Leonidaion

OLYMPIA

REMEMBER all you know about the Olympic Games:
- In honour of Zeus
- Began in 776 BC
- Every four years
- Sacred truce - severe penalties for breaking it
- For Greeks only
- No women allowed
- Events for men and boys only
- Special representatives sent by cities (eg. Athenian liturgies)

REMEMBER the story of Oinomaus:

King Oinomaus loved his daughter, Hippodameia, so much that he was determined not to lose her through marriage and, therefore, he required all possible suitors to race against him in a chariot. All losers were killed. According to one version of the story, if any suitor looked likely to win, Oinomaus killed him by throwing a spear from behind. In Classical times sightseers were shown a grave of thirteen unsuccessful suitors. Pelops of Phrygia, who gave his name to the Peloponnese, got the better of Oinomaus, by bribing Myrtilos, Oinomaus' groom who was also in love with Hippodameia, with the promise of one night with her. Myrtilos took the lynchpins out of Oinomaus' chariot and replaced them with wax. When Oinomaus' chariot got up speed, the wheels came off, Oinomaus was thrown from his chariot and killed. When Myrtilos demanded his rights, Pelops threw him into the sea. As he died he cursed Pelops and the curse rested on the whole house of Pelops (hence the death of Agamemnon, etc.).

There are also myths regarding Herakles and Olympia, claiming that Herakles marked out the site after sacking the city of Pisa, and held the first Olympic Games as a celebration.

THE OLYMPIC GAMES

The games were governed by the Olympian council, chosen from the aristocracy of Elis. Elis was the state in which Olympia was situated. The council met in the Bouleuterion and lived in the Prytaneion. There were numerous other officials.

The **Foot race** (Stadion) was earliest event, others added gradually over many years.

Ten months before the start of the Games, ten Umpires were chosen to supervise training, discipline and the events themselves.

Competitors trained for ten months, the last one at Olympia itself.

After each event, a herald announced the victor and gave him a palm.

On the last day, victors received a garland of wild olive.

Victors could erect a statue in the Altis (the sanctuary). If they won three events, the statue could have their own features.

There were great celebrations in the home city of a victor but competitors took part as individuals.

Victory odes were composed for some victors (see Odes of Pindar).

Day 1:- Procession to Olympia
        Oath not to cheat at altar of Zeus Horkeios in Bouleuterion
        Minor events for boys
Day 2:- Horse races and chariot races
        Pentathlon - which events?
Day 3:- Full Moon   - great sacrifice of 100 oxen
                    - banquet in evening
        Foot races - long distance, single
                            and double length
Day 4:- Wrestling, boxing, pankration
        Race in armour
Day 5:- Proclamation of victors
        Procession to temple of Zeus
        Feast for victors in Prytaneion

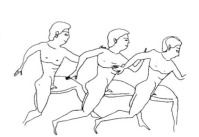

VISIT TO THE SITE

It is worthwhile exploring the site fully for, although many of the buildings are little more than foundations, it is possible to make sense of them.

THE PALAESTRA

Built in the 3rd century BC. It fits the description of a typical palaestra given by Vitruvius, the Roman writer on architecture.

LOOK FOR   Open court with Doric colonnade
            Water channels on all sides of court
            Rooms on three sides - Ionic porches or plain doorways
            Stone benches against walls
            On South, no rooms but double corridor
            On East & West, entrances with Corinthian columns

The next buildings have undergone many alterations both in construction and use. There was a priests' house, a hero shrine and later a Byzantine church. BUT most importantly here was discovered:-

THE WORKSHOP OF PHEIDIAS

In the shell of an early church.
Little to see but worth a visit for "I stood where Pheidias worked".
The workshop was identified by slivers of ivory & gold, terracotta moulds, tools and a jug inscribed on the base "I am Pheidias'".

LOOK FOR   the jug in the museum (it may be a fake!).

LEONIDAION

4th century BC hostel for distinguished visitors.
Adapted in 2nd century AD for Roman governor of Achaea.

LOOK FOR   Open court (with Doric colonnade)

IMAGINE   Rooms on all four sides
                Principal rooms on West
                Outside with Ionic colonnade

NOW ENTER THE ALTIS - the sanctuary of Zeus

BOULEUTERION

The building consisted of two apsidal halls with a court between.
It was altered and added to at various dates.

IMAGINE   The council meeting to organise the games
                Athletes swearing an oath not to cheat at statue of Zeus Horkeios

TEMPLE OF ZEUS

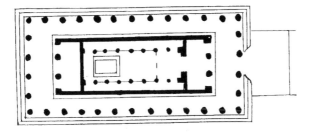

Architect was Libon of Elis (a local man).
Temple built between 470 & 456.
Destroyed in 6th century AD by earthquakes.

LOOK FOR   6×13 columns
                Embankment so that temple seems on a hill
                Crepidoma of 3 unequal steps
                Columns made of limestone with 3 rings at neck

IMAGINE   Size and height of temple
                Entablature - regular
                Pediments   - East - Oinomaus' chariot race
                             - West - Lapiths and Centaurs
                Acroteria - gilded bronze tripods on corners
                Roof - marble tiles and lion head waterspouts
                Metopes - Plain outside
                         - Labours of Herakles in pronaos & opisthodomos

INSIDE:-

LOOK FOR   Cella one step above stylobate
2 columns in antis - pronaos & opisthodomos
Position of statue between 5th & 7th columns

IMAGINE   Statue made by Pheidias
Two tier colonnade with viewing gallery at first floor level
Stone screens to keep away sightseers!

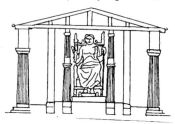

In front of the Temple of Zeus

LOOK FOR   Base of statue - **Nike of Paionios** (statue in is the museum)

IMAGINE   Statues on all the bases around the Altis (Pliny the Elder estimated
that there were 3000 statues in the sanctuary in his time - 70AD)

ECHO HALL

Also called Stoa Poikile from paintings which adorned it - 5th & 4th centuries BC.

LOOK FOR   Lead covered cramps - used for joining stones

REMEMBER   No mortar was used in Greek buildings

STADIUM

As in 4th century BC though the entrance vault is from the 2nd century BC.

NOTICE   Seats were only ever earth banks

IMAGINE   Trophies from battles displayed along the banks of the stadium -
probably on wooden poles. When these rotted, the trophies
were buried in improvements to the banks. The helmet of
Miltiades was found here (see museum). It was probably
dedicated after the battle of Marathon

LOOK FOR   Start and finish lines
Stone kerb
Water supply and basins
Paved area for judges
Altar opposite judges' enclosure - the only woman allowed to watch
the games (the priestess of Demeter) watched from this altar

As you leave the stadium:

ZANES

LOOK FOR   Bases for statues paid for by those caught cheating at the Games

IMAGINE   The statues - probably of Zeus striding forward with his thunderbolt

On your right:-

LOOK FOR   Foundations of treasuries, almost all from greater Greece

12 - Gela	8 - Altar of Gaia	4 - Epidamnus
11 - Megara	7 - Kyrene	3 - Samos
10 - Metapontum	6 - Sybaris	2 - Syracuse
9 - Selinus	5 - Byzantium	1 - Sikyon

LOOK FOR   Foundations of Metroon (temple of Mother Goddess - 4th century AD)

Beyond the treasuries

LOOK FOR   Remains of semi-circular Nymphaeum (160AD) of Herodes Atticus
                  (benefactor to Greece)

TEMPLE OF HERA

Earliest temple - so perhaps site originally sacred to an ancient mother goddess.
There was a festival to Hera with games at the sanctuary in which girls competed.
Dedication plaques were attached by girl winners to the columns of the temple.

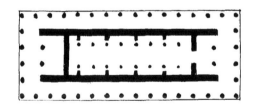
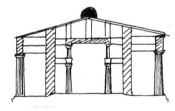

Originally built in early sixth century BC with wooden columns.
These were gradually replaced in stone as the wood rotted.
Built on limestone foundations with mud-brick above.
Mud-brick helped preserve base because eventually degenerated into mud covering.
Hermes of Praxiteles was found here under the mud.

LOOK AT   Capitals of various dates (which is which ??)
                  Cross walls (to help buttress cella walls or hold up the roof?)
                  Pedestal for statue of Zeus and Hera (head of Hera is in museum)
                  Base for Hermes of Praxiteles
                      (between columns 2&3 from East on N side)

Between Temples of Zeus and Hera

LOOK AT Grassy mound surrounded by stone slabs - shrine of Pelops

In front of and between Temple of Hera and shrine of Pelops

IMAGINE Great altar of Zeus (now a hole in the ground!)
Originally a huge heap of ashes, the remains of many sacrifices,
long since washed away by floods

Behind the Temple of Hera

LOOK AT Foundations of Philippeion - commissioned by Philip of Macedon
after his victory over the rest of Greece at Chaironea in 338 BC

LOOK FOR Remains of Prytaneion where officials lived and the feast for the
victors was held (a perpetual fire burnt here and its ashes were
added to the altar of Zeus)

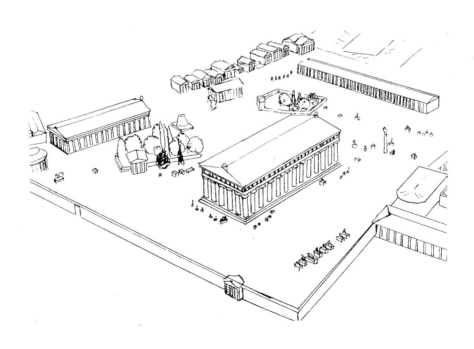

MUSEUM

The central hall is devoted to the sculptures of the Temple of Zeus, the other rooms
   follow a chronological sequence if you walk clockwise!!

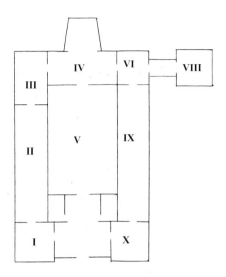

LOOK AT	**The model of the sanctuary in the entrance hall**
Room I	Early and Mycenaean Greece

Room II	Archaic - Temple of Hera
LOOK AT	**Archaic head of Hera** (or a sphinx) **Acroteria of temple of Hera**

Room III	Archaic
LOOK AT	Restored entablature and pediments of treasury of Megara (gods & giants) Terracotta pediment of treasury of Gela

Room IV	Early Classical and Classical
LOOK AT	**Zeus & Ganymede** (terracotta statuette) **Miltiades' helmet** Bronze helmet (booty from Persian war) **Nike of Paionios** made of Pentelic marble - thank offering for victory over Spartans from Messenians

Room V Sculpture of Temple of Zeus

CHARIOT RACE OF OINOMAUS AND PELOPS

The sculptures are arranged according to Pausanias' description and where they were found.

Zeus is in the centre (gods are always larger than humans).
To the left, as you look at it, is Oinomaus with his wife, Sterope.
To the right is Pelops with Hippodameia, the intended bride.

According to Susan Woodford:-
* Oinomaus looks confident as he explains the conditions for the race
* Pelops is withdrawn as he listens with his head modestly bowed
* Sterope is lost in her own thoughts with her arms anxiously folded
* Hippodameia adjusts her veil, and looks out

The sculptor has shown the calm before the storm with intense involvement of the main characters.
The attendants, by contrast, seem indifferent to the momentous event except ...
The seer who looks past the principal figures into the disastrous future before both heroes - his age is well portrayed in contrast to maturity of Pelops and youth of boy beside him (important as earliest portrayal of age in sculpture).
The lying figures represent rivers of Olympia, probably Kladeos - left, Alpheios - right.

BATTLE OF LAPITHS AND CENTAURS

At the wedding feast of Perithoos, the centaur guests became drunk and tried to carry off the Lapith women - a battle ensued!!

The centaurs are bestial and repulsive.
The battle represents epic struggle between man and untameable forces of nature.

Apollo is in the centre, the only still figure.
One of the heroes beside Apollo must be Perithoos, the other his friend, Theseus.
On Apollo's right is the bride, Deidameia, pushing an elbow into the centaur's face while pulling his hand away from her breast and at the same time removing his arm from round her waist. The centaur has his hoof round her thigh. She struggles but shows no emotion, according to Susan Woodford (perhaps not suitable for a queenly figure). Other figures show more emotion, especially a Lapith youth who wrinkles his brow as his lips part to emit a cry of pain while a centaur sinks his teeth into his arm.
The reclining figures are probably 4th century Pentelic marble replacements.

METOPES OF THE LABOURS OF HERAKLES

The traditional twelve labours originate from these

(many other labours are attributed to Herakles)

| Nemean Lion | Hydra of Lerna | Stymphalian Birds | Cretan Bull |

| Hind of Keryneia | Battle with Amazons | Erymanthean Boar | Mares of Diomedes |

| Geryon | Atlas and the Golden Apples | Fetching Kerberos from Hades | Augean Stables |

THINK OF   The problems of sculpture on metopes

LOOK AT   Use of diagonals and verticals and horizontals
How sculptor has filled the space

Room VI

LOOK AT   **Pheidias' wine cup** and tools from workshop
Clay moulds for statue making

Room VIII

LOOK AT   **Hermes of Praxiteles**   (is it really the original or a copy?)
Colour on right foot
Toolmarks on part of back (probably as result of later repair)
Shine on statue

Room IX & X

LOOK AT   Statuettes of athletes
Jumping weights

OLYMPIA TO TOLON

If you travel directly from Olympia to the great sites of the Argolid,
                Megalopolis and Nauplion are possible stopping-off points

Megalopolis
- Founded as centre for Arcadian Confederacy in 371 BC
- Forty villages moved their populations to form it
- City had a double wall five miles long
- Joined Confederacy of Achaia in 235 BC
- Sacked by Spartans in 223 BC
- Polybios, the historian, was born here about 200 BC

TO LOOK FOR
- Theatre (in danger of collapse) [Pausanias says it was the largest in Greece - 20000 spectators]
- Thersileon (assembly hall) for meetings of Arcadian Confederacy - 10000 members
- Stoa of Philip

Nauplion
- Fortified by Byzantines in 12th century AD
- Occupied by everyone - Franks, Turks and Venetians!!!
- Early capital of Modern Greece
- First king landed here in 1833

TO LOOK FOR
- Palamidi - fortress 700 feet up - built by Turks in 1711-4
- Bourdzi - Venetian fortress on an island -15th century

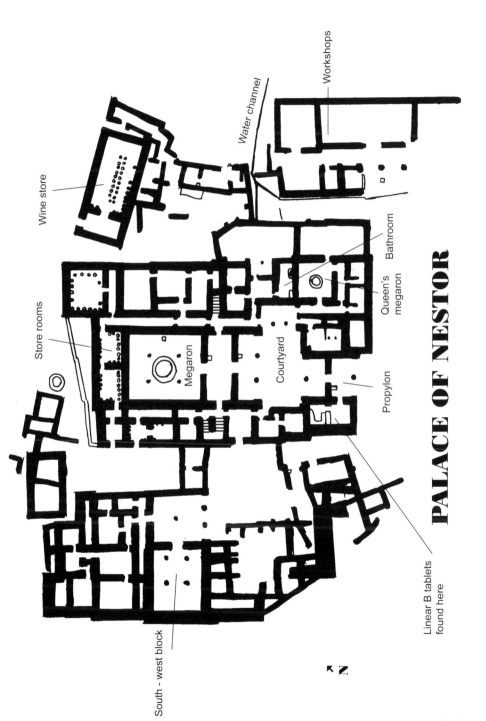

Wine store

Water channel

Workshops

Store rooms

Megaron

Queen's megaron

Bathroom

Courtyard

Propylon

South - west block

Linear B tablets found here

N

PALACE OF NESTOR

61

PALACE OF NESTOR

Mycenaean palace
Discovered 1939
Excavated since 1952

Not fortified
2 storeyed

Exterior walls – squared limestone blocks
Interior walls – rubble, plastered and frescoed
Upper walls – mud brick within wooden framework

REMEMBER Nestor - always ready to give advice
          - never at a loss for words
          - always ready to reminisce

> And now the Gerenian charioteer, Nestor, led Telemachus and Mentes, his sons and his daughters-in-law to his beautiful palace. When they had reached the royal palace, they sat down one after another on the seats and chairs. The old man mixed a bowl of sweet wine for them…..
>
> Odyssey III 386

PROPYLON (entrance gate)

LOOK FOR One column in front
      One column behind
      Door between

NOTICE   Columns had 64 flutes (Doric had 20, Ionic 24)

LOOK FOR Rooms on left where lots of Linear B tablets were found
         (Linear B = early form of Greek writing, used for records)

COURTYARD

On left
LOOK FOR Pantry which held wine jars and cups
      Waiting room with stuccoed benches

On right
LOOK FOR Column which supported balcony
      Queen's apartments beyond

Straight ahead
LOOK FOR Wide portico (2 columns *in antis*)
      Vestibule beyond

Now go into portico and vestibule

LOOK FOR Remains of staircase on right

When they had poured libations and drunk as much as they wanted, the rest went home to bed but Nestor let Telemachus sleep on a wooden bed under the echoing porch. The king himself slept at the back of the lofty house where the queen had prepared the bed and the bedding. When early rising, rosy-fingered Dawn came, Nestor got up from his bed, went out and sat on the glistening stones, which were in front of the lofty doors, all polished, white and shining.

Odyssey III 395

MEGARON

LOOK FOR   Ceremonial hearth (clay circle 4 metres in diameter)
Four bases of large columns which held galleried upper storey
Patterned floor – octopus but mostly abstract
Site of throne on right (depression in floor)
Channel from one hollow to another (for libations?)

IMAGINE   Frescoed walls (griffins and lions on walls behind throne)

REMEMBER Alcinous and Arete (king and queen of Phaeacians) in palace on Scherie

When you are in the shady halls and court, go quickly straight through the megaron until you reach my mother.

Odyssey VI 303

IMAGINE   Alcinous drinking wine like a god
Arete spinning wool dyed with sea-purple with her ladies sitting behind
Odysseus approaching and clasping Arete's knees

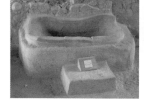

LOOK FOR   Store rooms – with large jars
Bathroom with terracotta tub

IMAGINE   Telemachus emerging from the bath.

When she had washed Telemachos and rubbed him with olive oil, she threw a tunic and a fine cloak around him and he stepped from the bath looking like the immortals.

Odyssey III 466

Return to courtyard

QUEEN'S MEGARON

LOOK FOR   Same rooms as main *megaron* but smaller
Room with drain hole (bathroom?)

Behind the car park

LOOK FOR   Tholos tomb
- partly reconstructed but an opportunity to look at the method of construction

CLASSICAL PYLOS

A good place to remember all you know about the Peloponnesian War (or to learn about one of the major events of the war!).

REMEMBER   Spartan military supremacy in the 6th century BC
The Persian wars
Growth of Athenian influence and power (through the Delian League)
Spartan irritation as they realised their influence was waning

REMEMBER   The inevitability of war between Athens & Sparta
Sparta – the power on land
Athens – the power on the sea
Sparta - the Oligarchy
Athens - the Democracy

REMEMBER   Pericles, the general - always gave good advice, according to Thucydides
Kleon, the populist - the first rabble-rouser in the Assembly

LOOK AT   the island of Sphakteria
the headland to the North

IMAGINE   the events of 425BC

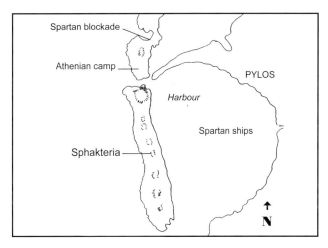

- Athenians on way to Sicily forced to shelter at Pylos because of storms
- Encouraged by Demosthenes (not the orator!) to fortify headland.
  (Demosthenes wanted an Athenian base on Spartan soil)
- Spartans arrived (part of the army had been besieging Athens) by land & sea
- Intended to block entrances to harbour but didn't
- Landed soldiers on island of Sphakteria to prevent Athenians doing so
- Blockaded base from the North
- Attacked Athenian base but failed to dislodge it
- Brasidas, the Spartan general, lost his shield - Athenians took it to Athens
  as a trophy

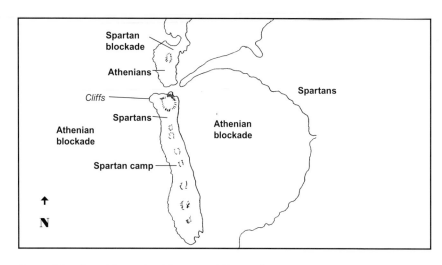

- Some Athenian ships arrived to support Demosthenes
- Entered harbour and attacked and destroyed Spartan ships
- Spartans now isolated on Sphakteria
- Stalemate so truce agreed
- Some Spartans taken to Athens to discuss end to war
- Spartans offered peace but Athenians demanded too much (urged on by Kleon)

So.....

- Stalemate continued — - Spartans blockaded by sea on Sphakteria
  - Athenians blockaded on land on headland
- Both sides in difficulties - not enough water on headland
  - no food on Sphakteria - supplies brought in secretly
- Kleon in Athens maintained it would be easy to dislodge Spartans on Sphakteria
- Nikias, the general, called his bluff; forced Kleon to command expedition to Pylos
- Accidental fire on Sphakteria destroyed woods and so....
- Enabled Athenians to see — - how many Spartans on the island
  - where to land on the island
- Kleon arrived
- Offered peace terms to the Spartans (they refused)
- Two days later, the Athenians attacked while it was still dark,
- Landed at the Southern end of the island
- Overwhelmed the Spartan lookout
- Then advanced on the main camp in the centre of the island
- Spartans resisted bravely but no space for their superior hoplite tactics
- Stalemate until Athenian allies scaled cliffs in North & surrounded Spartans.
- Spartans surrendered – unheard of before
- Spartan prisoners taken to Athens

Results

- No more annual Spartan attacks on Attica (prisoners used as hostages)
- Athenians even more over-confident because they had made Spartans surrender
- Kleon became more popular and powerful

SPARTA

SOCIETY
Spartiates – the full-time soldiers and citizens of Sparta.
Perioikoi (dwellers around) – expected to serve as soldiers but were not citizens.
Helots – slaves, descendants of the conquered Messenians.

REMEMBER   Sparta was the dominant military power in the 6th century BC
                Spartans were always afraid of a Helot revolt...
                        so they were never keen to venture far from home

GOVERNMENT
Only Spartiates could take part in government.
So an OLIGARCHY (rule by a few).
2 kings - military, religious & judicial functions.
Gerousia - Council of Elders.
Ephors - 5 overseers with great power.
Assembly of citizens - met once a month.

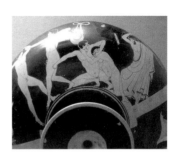

EDUCATION FOR BOYS
Only Spartiates underwent this training.
Plutarch says aim was to produce   quick obedience,
                                        ability to endure pain and hardship,
                                        courage and victory in battle.

Age 1-5   At home with mother and nurse
Age 6-12   Living in barracks with others of same age
               Learnt physical skills and to endure hardships
age 12-17   Learning soldiering but non-combat soldiers
               Trained to go barefoot (Xenophon says so that could run faster)
               One garment all the year round
               Given little food so that easy to go without
               Steal to supplement rations (Xenophon says to make them craftier)
Age 18-20   Drilled in huge school
               Captained by other youths (over 20 but not 30)
               Allowed to marry at 20 but   still lived in barracks
                                              visited wives secretly
Age 24-30   Front-line soldiers
               Great competition to be the best and to denounce others
Age 30   Eligible for assembly
               Now able to live at home but served as soldiers until age 60
               Still ate with fellow soldiers
               Grew hair to show physical strength

EDUCATION FOR GIRLS

Aim to produce healthy bodies to produce healthy citizens and mothers of heroes.
Lived at home but ... possibly organised into bands.
Exercised with boys in sports.
Took part in choral and dancing competitions - great rivalry.

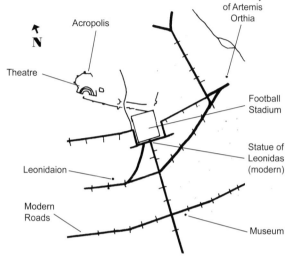

VISIT

Little remains of Greek city
In Roman times, the city was prosperous & had fine houses with mosaics

ACROPOLIS

LOOK FOR   Walls built between 267 and 386 AD

THEATRE

2nd or 1st century BC.
Only theatre at Megalopolis was bigger.

LOOK FOR   Tracks of movable stage building

SANCTUARY OF ARTEMIS ORTHIA

LOOK FOR   Altar on East
                 Temple on West
                 Theatre added in 2nd century AD

IMAGINE   Flogging of Spartan boys to test endurance
                 Spartan girls singing and dancing

LOOK FOR   Marble stelai inset with sickles   ) in honour of those
                 Inscribed altars   ) who passed the test!

LEONIDAION

Originally small 3rd century temple

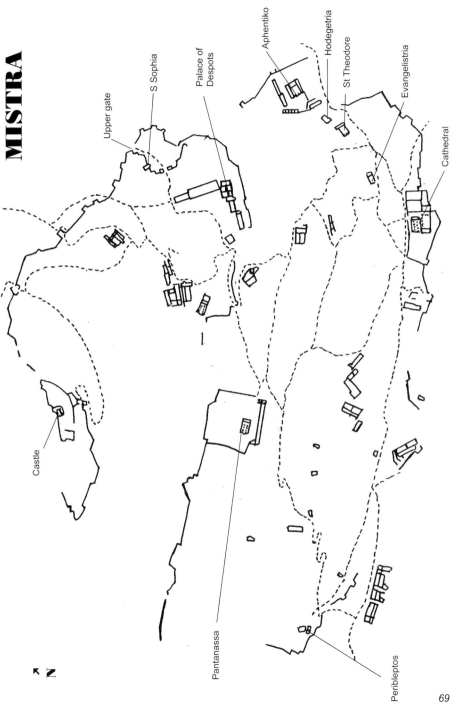

MISTRA

Castle

Upper gate

S Sophia

Palace of Despots

Aphentiko

Hodegetria

St Theodore

Evangelistria

Cathedral

Pantanassa

Peribleptos

N

MISTRA

3 miles West of Sparta

1249	Franks built castle to check Slav raiders (first occupation)
	Soon under Byzantine control and city developed
1460	Surrendered to Turks but still prospered
1687	Venetian control (silk production main source of revenue)
	City population 42000
1715	Turks controlled again (second largest place in Peloponnese)
1770	Looted by Greeks and burned by Turks
1825	Destroyed by Turks

Castle at top of city
City in two parts below:
> Upper housed aristocratic families in Byzantine times
> Lower had cathedral, monasteries and houses

UPPER GATE

SANTA SOPHIA
The palace church

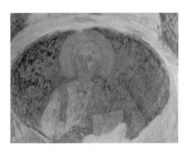

LOOK FOR   Pantokrator (the Almighty) in the apse
                     Nativity etc. in the side chapel

WATER CISTERN

PALACE OF DESPOTS
Large building complex
Built between 13th and 15th centuries

MONASTERY OF OUR LADY PANTANASSA
Built 1365 but enlarged 1428

LOOK FOR   Loggia/porch with view over valley

ST THEODORE
Built 1290

LOOK FOR   Octagonal shape
                     Wall paintings

CHURCH OF OUR LADY HODEGETRIA

Built 1310

LOOK FOR   4 small domes round central dome
                  Beautiful bell tower

Inside
LOOK FOR   Tomb of Theodore II
                  Paintings

CATHEDRAL - ST DEMETRIOS

Early 14th century.
Upper part replaced in early 15th century with cross in square form (five domes).

LOOK FOR   Outer porch, belfry and North portico
                  Basilica form with three aisles
                  Capitals with leaf pattern (early Byzantine)
                  Screen (restored in mid and late Byzantine times)
                  Bishop's throne (17th century)
                  Paintings – earliest in North aisle
                  Double-headed eagle in marble on floor
                        - where the last Byzantine emperor was crowned

CHURCH OF OUR LADY EVANGELISTRIA

Another church
Cross in square (end of 14th century)

MONASTERY OF OUR LADY PERIBLEPTOS

LOOK FOR   Frescoes   Pantokrator in dome
                                    Ascension
                                    Nativity
                                    Transfiguration

MYCENAE

THINK OF   Agamemnon's palace
Homer   "Mycenae rich in gold"
         "well-built"
         "broad-streeted"
Aeschylus - Agamemnon's murder

2000 BC Summit of hill fortified but little else
1500 BC Shaft graves - much gold "Mask of Agamemnon"
1350 BC Huge walls, palace culture - also many smaller houses within walls
1250 BC Walls enlarged to enclose shaft graves
          Lion Gate
1200 BC Walls extended to enclose water supply
          Soon after ... destruction by fire
1100 BC Palace abandoned but site still inhabited (small houses not palace)
 400 BC Argos controlled Mycenae and destroyed some of fortifications
 150 AD Pausanias visited Mycenae and described it

Mycenae was first explored in modern times by Heinrich Schliemann who was convinced that the stories of Homer were in some sense true. He first excavated (bulldozed!) Troy but did find evidence of the Bronze age inhabitants. In 1876 he came to Mycenae and very soon found the famous gold mask on display in the National Museum. He sent a telegram to the King of Greece: "I have gazed on the face of Agamemnon" - in fact the gold mask is of earlier date than Agamemnon.

As we approach from the modern village ...

LOOK DOWN RIGHT   To see remains of Mycenaean bridge

THE SITE

NOTICE   Position of site with steep ravines on two sides (good defences)

LION GATE

LOOK AT   Earliest monumental sculpture in Europe
         Size of stone blocks - lintel and threshold each weigh over 20 tons
         Squared stones in wall here
           - elsewhere rough but cleverly fitted together
         Walls here make it easy to attack invaders - attack from the side
         Lions - with paws on joined altars and column of building between
                  (notice that the column is tapered like a Minoan column
                        - narrower at bottom than top)
           - heads were separate - perhaps semi-precious stone

LOOK FOR   Holes in threshold at inner angle of uprights for hinges
         Holes in jambs for wooden bolts (most other holes later in date)

Inside the walls it is not easy to make sense of the excavations - lots of ruins of walls!!!
Nevertheless some things can be made out ...

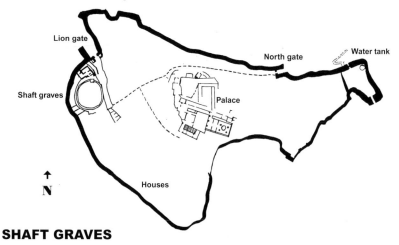

SHAFT GRAVES

Grave Circle A - there is another circle outside the walls near the car park.
Site of Schliemann's first excavations - six royal graves and several lesser ones.

REMEMBER   The "mask of Agamemnon" from the National Museum

CLIMB to the top of the hill to see ...

THE PALACE

This has the standard layout of Mycenaean/Minoan palaces so ...

IMAGINE   Odysseus's palace on Ithaca
                The suitors feasting

The grand staircase entrance (1) has disappeared down the hill
There was another entrance at (5)

IMAGINE   Agamemnon climbing these stairs on his return
                from Troy and entering ante-room (2),
                great court (3) followed by throne room (4).

NOTICE   Throne room had 4 columns to support roof + a hearth in centre

IMAGINE   Agamemnon going to his bath - room 6 is suggested if you can
                find it - it is sunken and has/had a red plaster floor!

On the summit of the hill a temple was built in Classical times
                               - just to confuse later visitors!!!

WALK over the summit of the hill to the Easternmost corner of the fortifications

LOOK AT   The postern gate

If you have a torch ... or can attach yourself to someone else who has ...

CLIMB DOWN   The narrow staircase through a small entrance

TO SEE   The tank providing a safe water supply to the fortress (1200BC)
             Pipes brought the water from springs outside the fortress

RETURN   To the entrance via the North Gate, if possible

Outside the walls

LOOK AT   The tomb of Clytemnestra (a tholos tomb) - forgotten by Hellenistic
                 times because a theatre was built on top
             Grave Circle B - 14 royal graves - possibly early than Circle A

MUSEUM
Well worth a visit.

LOOK AT   The model of the site
             Remains from the Shaft graves
             Linear B tablets

TREASURY OF ATREUS

There are over 100 similar tombs all over Greece.
Nine at Mycenae.
This one dates from about 1250BC.
Pausanias thought these tombs were treasuries, hence the name.

LOOK AT   Size of stones in the approach (dromos)
             Lintel (weight about 120 tons)

ESTIMATE   Height of doorway as your enter ...

LOOK AT   Overlapping stones forming cone (not really a dome)
             Small chamber on right where corpse was placed

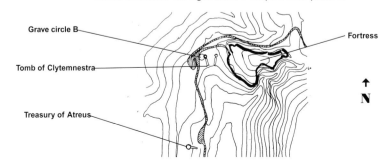

TOLON TO ATHENS

Diolkos   - Slipway for dragging ships between Corinthian & Saronic Gulfs
                 - Avoided long and dangerous voyage round the south of the
                       Peloponnese

Megara   - Very small city-state
                - Important in Peloponnesian War

Eleusis   - see page 85

Daphni
11th century Byzantine church on the Sacred Way from Athens to Eleusis

NOTICE   Built in shape of Greek cross - all arms same length

MOSAICS   The positions of the mosaics are as usual in Byzantine churches
                   (compare with Osios Loukas):

                  In the dome is Christ in Glory (heaven) surrounded by archangels

                  Below are the prophets and apostles

                  In the centre of the apse is the Virgin and Child

                  Also on this level are scenes from the life of Christ

                  Below this, we reach the earth with saints, monks, etc.

TIRYNS

On rock only 85 feet above the plain of Argos.
Myth said built with the aid of the Cyclops.
Diomedes was king at time of the Trojan War.

Dates from 2500 BC
Present structure about 1400 - 1200 BC

The entrance is on the East side.

CLIMB the wide ramp

As you turn sharp left

LOOK FOR   The lower fortress

NOTICE   Thickness of the walls
                 Good defensive position

Outer gate

Middle gate

Queen's apartments

Megaron

Forecourt

Great Propylaia

East gallery
Storerooms

King's court

Pass the Outer Gate and
You will soon reach the Middle Gate

LOOK AT   Threshold and lower half of door posts with bolt holes.

Pass through Middle Gate and Inner Gate to reach the Forecourt:

First FOLLOW modern stairs down to East gallery (storerooms
        in the thickness of the walls) - the walls have been well polished
        by countless sheep in the past thousand years!

Then on returning to the forecourt:

TURN RIGHT   Through Great Propylaia:

Just inside the first door:

LOOK RIGHT   Down the corridor which leads to the Queen's apartments.

LOOK AHEAD   To the Great Court.

TURN RIGHT   Into King's court   - surrounded by colonnade
                                     - altar on right just inside

LOOK AT   The megaron as at Mycenae with place for throne on East wall

LOOK FOR   Bathroom on West side - its floor is one slab of limestone & there
                                     is a drain in one corner.
                 Stairs to outside (a well outside)

EPIDAUROS

The Sacred Grove of Asklepios has boundary stones all around it. Inside the sanctuary, no men die and no women bear children because the religious law is the same as on the island of Delos.

Pausanias

SANCTUARY OF ASKLEPIOS

Asklepios was the son of Apollo and a nymph, brought up by Chiron the centaur from whom he learnt the art of healing.

Originally the sanctuary at Epidauros was sacred to Apollo (there is an altar above the theatre) but during the sixth and fifth centuries Asklepios was associated with Apollo and in the fourth century BC Asklepios succeeded Apollo.

The sanctuary belonged to the city of Epidauros and the citizens elected the annual priest and his assistants and officials.

This sanctuary was one of **healing**:

- A visitor purified himself
- Made sacrifices
- Performed tests/rituals prescribed by the priests
- Slept in the **abaton** wrapped in the skin of the sacrificed animal
- Hoped for a cure (or instructions for a cure) in a dream that night.

Recovered patients gave expensive gifts and votive offerings to the sanctuary.

There are numerous examples of cures recorded in inscriptions:

> Kleio had been pregnant for five years but had not given birth to a child. In despair, she went to Epidauros and slept in the abaton. The next day, when she left the sanctuary she gave birth to a baby boy. As soon as he was born, the child got up, walked to the fountain, bathed and then went back to his mother. Kleio wrote on the votive stele: "Do not be amazed at the size of this stele, but at the greatness of the god, Kleio had been pregnant for five years, but then she slept in the abaton and the god healed her".

> Heraieus from Mytilene was completely bald. He also slept in the abaton. The god rubbed ointment onto his head, and in the morning Heraieus woke up with plenty of hair on his head.

> One day a blind man, to whom Asklepios had restored his sight, refused to give a gift to thank the god for his cure. Asklepios therefore deprived him of his sight immediately. When the miser returned to the sanctuary and begged to be forgiven, he promised not to repeat the insult. So, the god took pity on him and gave him back his sight - but only in one eye!

In later centuries, the cures less miraculous and more based on medical treatments.

Every 4 years there was an athletic & musical festival - 9 days after Isthmian Games.

THE THEATRE

A good example of a Greek theatre - Built into hillside like most Greek theatres
                                                - Not freestanding like most Roman theatres
                                                - Circular orchestra

Tradition says built by Polykleitos the Younger
                                         (mid 4th century BC) but probably a little later.

Upper block added in 2nd century BC.

LOOK AT	14000 seats 55 rows Lower block has 12 sections, upper 23 Seats of honour made of red stone Ordinary seats of white limestone
LOOK AT	Orchestra of beaten earth Altar in centre Gutter for rainwater in front of seats
GO TO	The very top of the theatre
LISTEN	To sounds made in the orchestra. The acoustics of the theatre are particularly good and you can hear a whisper anywhere (if there aren't too many extraneous noises!!)

> The Epidaurians have a theatre in their sanctuary which seems to me particularly worth a visit. The Roman theatres excel all the others in the world: the theatre at Megalopolis in Arkadia is unique for its size: but who can begin to rival Polykleitos for the beauty and composition of his architecture? He was the one who built the theatre and the round building, called the tholos.
>
> Pausanias

THE MUSEUM

LOOK AT	Inscriptions recording miraculous cures Details of temple of Artemis - dog & boar's head gutter spouts Ionic columns from **Abaton** Details of the **Tholos** (not very reliable)

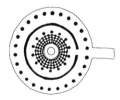

After leaving the museum ...FOLLOW THE PATH ...to visit the sanctuary

It is rather a jumble of ruins but it is worth a short tour.

REMEMBER all the details in the museum when you look at the sanctuary.

THE SANCTUARY

Pass the **Katagogeion** (a hostel for important visitors to the Festival - just an impressive set of foundations of cloistered courts each surrounded by 18 rooms. It originally had two storeys.

THE GYMNASIUM

Really a feasting building for the Festival

LOOK FOR   Stone supports for couches in some rooms (space for 11 couches)
                        3 halls for larger numbers
                        Monumental entrance (base reconstructed) on North side
                        Roman Odeion built inside it

THE STADIUM

LOOK AT   Drains at side
                        Start/finish lines
                        Seats partly cut in rock

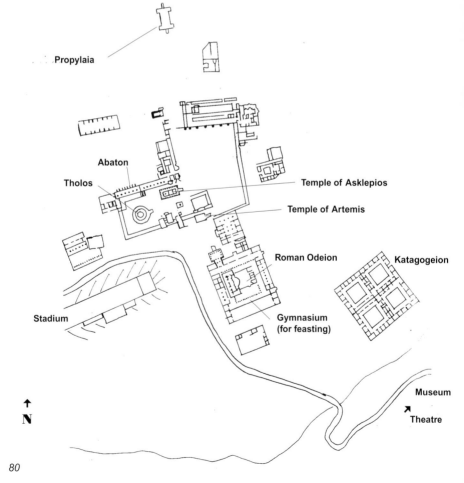

THE THOLOS

Called the Thymele in the inscriptions.
Built by Polykleitos the Younger (360-320 BC).
It cost 50 talents to build - twice as much as the temple of Asklepios (a great deal).

LOOK AT   The concentric walls - what was their purpose? - snake pit? or?...

NOTICE   Modern reconstruction

IMAGINE   26 Doric columns of limestone - stuccoed & painted
                   Window on each side of door
                   Interior colonnade of 14 marble Corinthian columns
                   Floor of black and white marble
                   Ceiling coffered, carved and painted (remember museum)
                   Lion's head gargoyles on roof (water spouts)
                   Floral acroterion (decoration on top of roof)

A round construction of white stone called the **tholos** has been built nearby. It is well worth a visit.
Inside is a picture by Pausias in which Eros has thrown away his bow and arrows, and carries a lyre
instead. "Drunkenness" is also there, painted by Pausias, drinking from a wine-glass; you can see
a wine-glass in the painting and a woman's face through it. In my day six of the stone tablets which
stood in the enclosure are left, though there were more in antiquity. The names of men and women
healed by Asklepios are engraved on them, with the diseases and how they were healed.

                                                                       Pausanias

THE ABATON

LOOK AT   Stoas (colonnades) where patients slept while waiting for a cure
                       or for instructions on how to obtain a cure
                   Benches for patients
                   Two storeys at West end
                   Single storey at East end
                   Sacred well in SW corner

TEMPLE OF ASKLEPIOS

Architect was Theodotos; Timotheus provided the models for the pediment sculpture.
An inscription tells us that it took 4 years 8 months to build and cost 24 talents.

LOOK FOR   Ramp for approach (as at Aegina)

IMAGINE   6×11 Doric columns
                   Doors made of ivory
                   Statue of Asklepios as described by Pausanias

The statue of Asklepios is half the size of Olympian Zeus at Athens, and made of ivory and gold; the
inscription says it was made by Thrasymedes of Paros, son of Arignotos. Asklepios sits on a throne
holding a staff, with one hand over the serpent's head, and a dog lying beside him. The carvings on
the throne show the deeds of Argive divine heroes, Bellerophon and the Chimaira, and Perseus taking
the head of Medusa. Near the temple is the place where the suppliants of the god go to sleep.

                                                                       Pausanias

THE TEMPLE OF ARTEMIS

IMAGINE   Reconstruction as you saw it in the museum

THE PROPYLAIA

LOOK FOR   Monumental entrance (only the base remains)

CORINTH

Its position on the isthmus was very important but, because the isthmus is nearly four miles across, Corinth needed a large population to control it. There were harbours on both gulfs (Saronic and Corinthian).

Acrocorinth was the only suitable Acropolis but it was really only useful as a place of refuge not for occupation.

Corinth was always important as a trading city. It was famed for its wealth and luxury - hence the thousand prostitutes at the temple of Aphrodite on Acrocorinth.

St Paul spent eighteen months in Corinth, working and preaching. He was accused by the Jewish community before the Roman authorities of corrupting their faith.

700 BC   Corinth was an important city - trade, art, etc.

500 BC   Athens became pre-eminent and Corinth was less powerful

338 BC   Philip of Macedon chose Corinth for his Conference of Greek states -
Greece was no longer a series of independent states

146 BC   Destroyed by the Romans for mistreating its envoys

44 BC   Refounded by Julius Caesar - colonists from Italy + freed slaves

27 BC   Became capital of Province of Achaea (reorganisation of Augustus)

267, 365, 551 etc. etc. - ravaged by barbarians, earthquakes, etc. until 1858, after
another earthquake, New Corinth was built elsewhere!

SO   **Corinth** is a ROMAN city with a few Greek features

It is not easy to make sense of the site ... so ...

LOOK AT   Temple of Apollo

NOTICE   Typical 6th century temple
- 6×15 columns
- limestone
- squat columns
- wide capitals

LOOK AT   Stucco on underside of fallen column

LOOK AT   Fountain of Peirene
Bema (platform where St Paul addressed the Roman court)
Museum
Theatre - outside the site across the road/car park

If we have time and you wish

EXPLORE the site using the detailed plan!!

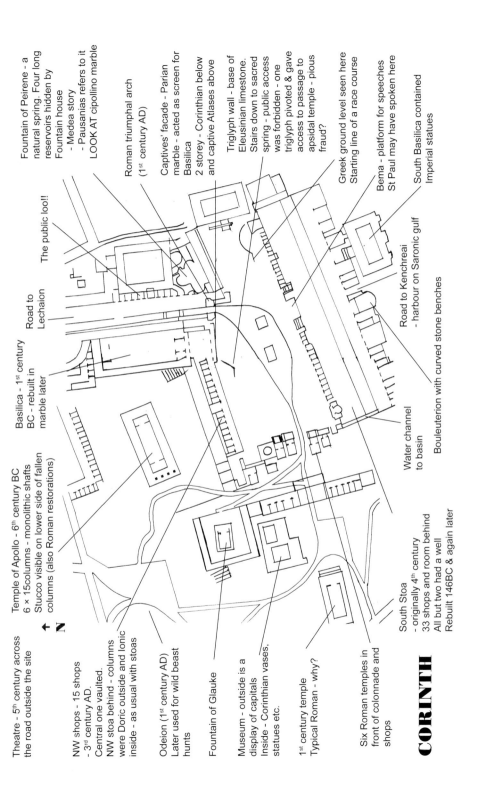

CORINTH

Theatre - 5th century across the road outside the site

NW shops - 15 shops - 3rd century AD. Central one vaulted. NW stoa behind - columns were Doric outside and Ionic inside - as usual with stoas

Odeion (1st century AD) Later used for wild beast hunts

Fountain of Glauke

Museum - outside is a display of capitals Inside - Corinthian vases, statues etc.

1st century temple Typical Roman - why?

Six Roman temples in front of colonnade and shops

South Stoa - originally 4th century 33 shops and room behind All but two had a well Rebuilt 146BC & again later

Temple of Apollo - 6th century BC 6 × 15 columns - monolithic shafts Stucco visible on lower side of fallen columns (also Roman restorations)

← N

Road to Lechaion

The public loo!!

Basilica - 1st century BC - rebuilt in marble later

Water channel to basin

Bouleuterion with curved stone benches

Road to Kenchreai - harbour on Saronic gulf

Fountain of Peirene - a natural spring. Four long reservoirs hidden by Fountain house
- Medea story
- Pausanias refers to it
LOOK AT cipollino marble

Roman triumphal arch (1st century AD)

Captives' facade - Parian marble - acted as screen for Basilica
2 storey - Corinthian below and captive Atlases above

Triglyph wall - base of Eleusinian limestone. Stairs down to sacred spring - public access was forbidden - one triglyph pivoted & gave access to passage to apsidal temple - pious fraud?

Greek ground level seen here Starting line of a race course

Bema - platform for speeches St Paul may have spoken here

South Basilica contained Imperial statues

ATTICA

Thebes
Plataia
Mount Kithairon
Mount Parnes
Phyle •
Dekeleia
Rhamnous
Marathon
Eleusis
Megara
Athens
Salamis
Mount Hymettos
Brauron
Aegina
Thorikos
Laurion
Sounion

SOUNION

A landmark for sailors approaching Athens.
One of few sanctuaries of Poseidon.
60 metres above the sea.
Temple built of local white marble.

LOOK AT   Propylaia (Entrance gate) on North side in line with east end of temple
                     Terrace wall on North and West of temple
                     Platform between temple and sea for worshippers

TEMPLE OF POSEIDON

44×102 feet
6×13 columns   20 feet high
                  3'3" diameter (very slender)
                  16 flutes
Frieze inside pronaos showed Theseus, Gods and giants, Lapiths and centaurs!

LOOK AT   Lord Byron's graffito on South east anta (at base of a block)

Temple of Athena was ½ kilometre to North on low hill on isthmus.
It was "improved" in the fifth century BC.

ELEUSIS

REMEMBER all you know about the Mysteries
- Festival of Demeter
- Initiation essential and only for spiritually fit
- Only for Greeks but for men, women and slaves
- 55 day truce to allow safe access
- Trip to Piraeus for purification with piglet in the sea
- Procession to Eleusis

The present surroundings are really attractive!!!

THE SITE
The sanctuary was in use for over 1000 years so it underwent many changes.

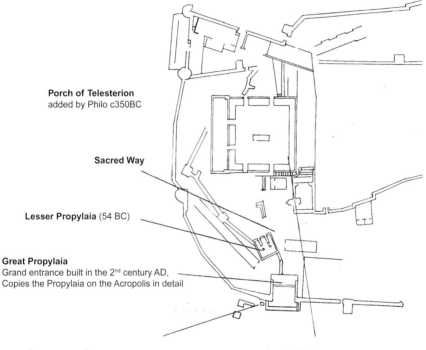

Porch of Telesterion
added by Philo c350BC

Sacred Way

Lesser Propylaia (54 BC)

Great Propylaia
Grand entrance built in the 2nd century AD,
Copies the Propylaia on the Acropolis in detail

6th century well
where Demeter is supposed
to have been found mourning the loss
of her daughter, Persephone (Kore)

TELESTERION
The sanctuary building
expanded many times to
reach present size by Pericles' time

IMAGINE   In the Telesterion, anaktoron in centre - on its top burnt the sacred fire
6×7 rows of columns supporting the roof
8 tiers of seats on each side
6 doors
3000 initiates at the Festival
"Things said, things done, things revealed"

AEGINA

On the journey
LOOK FOR   Piraeus with its three harbours

On the ferry trip
LOOK FOR   Acrocorinth in distance on mainland

Aegina was occupied in Mycenaean times
7th-6th centuries   Prosperous from trade
                    First European city to mint coins - turtles
                    Rivalry with Athens
5th century   Fought at Salamis & Plataia but had wanted to yield to Persia.
457 BC   Besieged and crushed by Athens
431 BC   Inhabitants expelled and island colonised by Athenians
403 BC   Exiles returned but never again great power

1826 AD   First capital of liberated Greece

On our trip to the temple of Aphaia, we may pass
                    Capital of island from 9th century AD till 1826 (Palaiokhora)
                        destroyed and rebuilt twice
                    Ruined castle on summit
                    Ruins of more than 20 churches
                    Monastery
                    Pistachio trees

TEMPLE OF APHAIA

The temple was built for a local goddess, Britomartis. She was fond of hunting and, therefore, was especially favoured by Artemis. King Minos fell in love with her and she tried to escape his clutches by jumping into the sea. She was caught in a fishing net and a sailor fell in love with her. She escaped, swam away to Aegina and hid in a cave in an ancient sanctuary. So she was called Aphaia (the vanished one).

In the fifth century, Aphaia seems to have been equated with Athena and so Athena appears on the two pediments

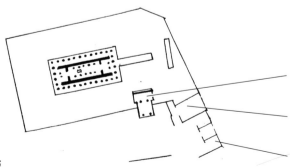

The temple was built on an
    artificial terrace

Grand entrance built in
5th century

Feasting rooms for festival
visitors

Also, baths for purification

The temple was built in the first few years of the fifth century.

It shows many signs of "modern" ideas, i.e. slender columns, upright abacus, pronaos and opisthodomos but presumably the priests were unhappy about the lack of an adyton, as a door was knocked through the back wall of the cella and grilles were placed between the opisthodomos columns to form an adyton. In order to damage as few stones as possible and to make the cutting easier, the door is slightly off-centre.

LOOK FOR (if possible)   Continuous taper of internal two-tier columns
Marks of grilles on entrance columns - hard to make out
Off-centre door to adyton
U-grooves in entablature for lifting stones
Altar and ramp
Gap between columns - are all equal or do gaps vary?
Join between shaft and echinus - what is it like?
Traces of coloured stucco
Cella floor was red stucco, also columns etc. coloured
Stones lying around with grooves and holes for lifting

REMEMBER   Sculpture from pediments is in a museum in Munich
(the British had the wrong date for the auction!)
West pediment was earlier & showed later Sack of Troy
by Agamemnon
East pediment was a little later & showed the first Sack
of Troy by Herakles

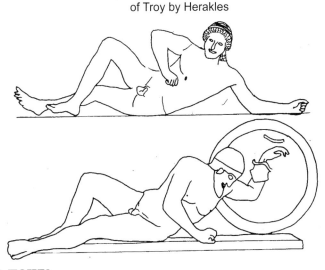

AEGINA TOWN

Harbour corresponds to ancient trading harbour; military harbour was to North
- remains of quays may be visible there under water.
Museum has inscriptions from temple of Aphaia.
Excavations largely of Mycenaean settlement.
but   temple of Apollo c 520 BC
circular structure may be tomb of Phokos (Pausanias)

Have you seen?

Where?

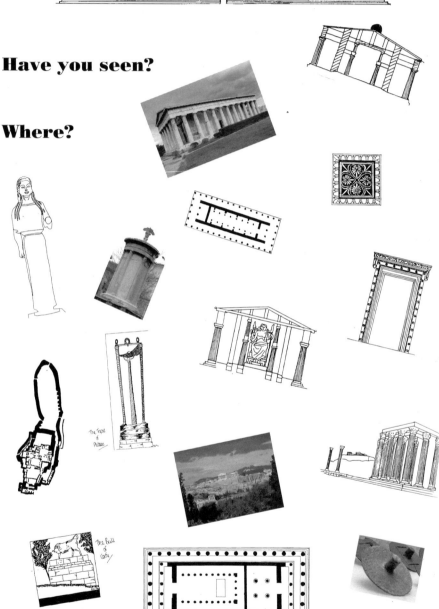